The Limits of Politics

Collective Goods and Political Change in Postindustrial Societies

Roger Benjamin

The University of Chicago Press

Chicago and London

To Alison

The University of Chicago Press, Chicago 60637
The University of Chicago Press, Ltd., London

Printed in the United States of America
84 83 82 81 80   5 4 3 2 1

ROGER BENJAMIN is professor of political science at the University of Minnesota and coauthor of *Patterns of Political Development: Japan, India, Israel.*

Library of Congress Cataloging in Publication Data

Benjamin, Roger W
The limits of politics.

Bibliography: p.
Includes index.
1. Political sociology. 2. Public goods.
3. Comparative government. 4. Social change.
I. Title.
JA76.B42   301.5'92   79-19473
ISBN 0-226-04233-2

The Limits of Politics

Contents

Preface

I argue in this essay that redesign of political institutions is necessary, in fact inevitable, in societies that have moved "beyond development," into the postindustrial phase of sociopolitical change. I reach this conclusion through two main steps. First, I try to show that we must be alert to a new set of structural (threshold) changes now transforming the economic, social, and political systems of the set of societies often labeled Western or advanced industrial, i.e., those of Western Europe, North America (excluding Mexico), and Japan. Second, I develop a model of government based on collective goods theory to interpret the political implications of the structural changes identified. I then examine the implications of my argument in a number of design-relevant public policy topics facing postindustrial societies: value change, the changing nature of "development" itself, and the usefulness of principles of centralization design for local government and the nation-state.

The work which follows provides the detailed argument leading to the conclusion that redesign of political institutions is crucial, but I shall note some of the main points here. In the economy of postindustrial societies, there is a threshold shift; at the peak of industrialization, manufacturing and related industrial activities account for a greater proportion of the economy than do agriculture and the service sector. In the societies that are entering the postindustrial phase, the service sector is rapidly supplanting industry in dominance. Central to the service sector is the increased importance of information itself as the primary cost absorbed in individual and group activity. In fact the search for the solution becomes more costly—in time as well as money—than the solution itself. Moreover, in these postindustrial societies there is increased interdependence in all aspects of life. While our strategy for the information problem entails the development of greater interdependence through the creation of systems that attempt to provide linkages between individuals and groups, this interdependence is itself the cause of substantial increases in negative externalities, i.e., unwanted spillover effects generated in the production and/or consumption of goods which citizens must absorb. An increase in the consumption of irreplaceable natural resources, water and air pollution, too much city traffic, excessive numbers of phone contacts by salespersons, etc., lead citizens to collective action. Usually this involves an effort to get government assistance in achieving redress to provide relief from the good in question. In addition, growth of the service sector itself brings a substantial rise in public service and regulation. I shall argue below that once a minimally sufficient material standard of living and the construction of essential social institutions for health care, education, and welfare are achieved, individual attention naturally turns to qualitatively different concerns. The quality of the good (service) delivered becomes the issue, not the mere presence of the institution designed to deliver it.

This rise in the public service and regulation sector, plus the changing focus of its activities, is especially important. For one thing, as industry loses ground to the public sector, it becomes more difficult to operate the economy by the standard measures of productivity, cost and efficiency. Most human service occupations are such that actual increases in productivity (as measured by classical economic measures) are sporadic or nonexistent. A welfare officer probably provides more efficient service (as measured by the quality of his performance) when he has fewer cases to handle. In addition, in the absence of the market mechanism, there are no internal ways to avoid an inexorable rise in costs, both of wages and materials, which seldom remain constant or decline. Such conditions, I argue, lead to the need to redefine both the nature of the service sector, including the public, and the way we measure the quality of the services rendered. It is no accident, for example, that collective bargaining and strikes are growing exponentially in the public sector, where the absence of meaningful comparative performance indicators leaves a group's relative strength in collective action as the only powerful criterion distinguishing postal workers from university professors. We have lived usefully with a set of economic concepts and measures that were developed during the period of industrialization. We are now faced with new problems and must develop a different set of measures of economic performance.

A rise in the demand for public provision of goods and services continues in the societies I am writing about, and yet there is also increasing agreement about the existence of upper limits to the public sector—either in its entirety or parts thereof. Even if one is not prepared to accept the argument that there are total upper limits to this sector, most observers agree that the extraordinary increases in expenditures (as a proportion of the GNP) for particular services such as local government, health, and social security are declining or will soon do so.

All this stimulates heightened debate, but there is perhaps another trend that, if I have analyzed it accurately, will lead to an inevitable growth in political conflict. This trend concerns the increase in numbers and importance of collective goods occupying a central place in economic and political activity. Economists have distinguished public from private goods. If private goods are those bought and sold in the marketplace where the laws of supply and demand apply, public goods are those services that must be provided by some larger or central authority for defense, community well-being, law and order, etc. Roads, bridges, and welfare are often called public goods, goods which in theory if not in practice are indivisible: if provided to one member of the community, they cannot be denied to any other particular member. Between public goods—about whose existence there is little debate—and divisible private goods (those produced for and consumed by individuals who presumably have chosen specific items on which they prefer to expend their resources) are collective goods which have significant negative as well as positive spillover effects. A good deal of confusion and debate about these goods is reflected in uncertainty over nomenclature and conceptual and empirical meaning. There is agreement that undesirable side effects of goods produced by government, such as nuclear or coal energy plants, may be treated as negative externalities and hence come under the collective goods category. It is equally accepted in 1980 that citizens may treat cigarette smoke as a negative externality, and thus laws are enacted to regulate smoking, which was treated as a private good in the past. There is a great deal of debate over collective goods concerning who should pay what proportion of a good's cost to whom and who should consume any possible externalities attached to it. Increasingly, citizens resort to collective action either to demand provision of one good or to ward off the unwanted consequences of another. Their action is inevitably directed at government.

Finally, more citizens than before in postindustrial societies have an adequate material standard of living and are better educated. This means they are free to pursue a set of goods recently classified as positional in nature. Goods such as national parks or proverbial small South Sea islands are distinctly finite in number, but the people who wish to enjoy these goods are not. Excessive numbers of automobiles in large cities contribute to a decline in their worth; any good of this type which is zero sum in nature will lead to increased political conflict. Both positional and collective goods are growing in postindustrial societies, and this gives credence to a predicted rise in associated political conflict.

The point of all this is that if construction and change of largely centralized social-economic and political institutions are the hallmark of the industrial era, efforts to cope with the effects of these changes, human services, and the redesign of these institutions describe the present and future in postindustrial societies. Redesign rather than decentralization is called for, because the debate over centralization of governmental institutions is miscast. It is a question of matching the size of the government unit with the good to be delivered, public or collective, and linking these to the catchment (community) appropriate for consumption of the good. Because publics are more diverse and better educated, their wants are also more diverse. This suggests that equal diversity in the design of political institutions is required. In addition, there are a number of other implications of the argument relevant to political and public policy.

What follows, then, is a model of the political impact of a constellation of social-economic changes which makes for a qualitatively different set of issues on the local and national public policy agendas in the societies covered. Renewed political participation (though of the "non-normal," i.e., nonvoting-related type) and a rise in political conflict (though again of a different character from that in the past) are among the major themes of this essay. Like any model, my argument serves to highlight one dimension of reality and thus does not give a balanced vision of other equally important dimensions. For instance, in many of the societies from which this work is drawn, aspects of postindustrialization overlie or are interwoven with areas and problems of industrialization. For many, an adequate material standard of living is still a dream. For many, especially the working classes, achievement of mature industrialization itself apparently brought not greater economic and social equality but, rather, greater inequality. The issue of social equality becomes very important in the postindustrial phase of change.

I have alluded to concepts from collective goods theory. I hope to show how this set of analytics can provide a powerful theory base from which we can significantly advance our understanding of the social-economic and political world we live in.

Acknowledgments

I gratefully acknowledge support, both institutional and personal, without which this book would not have been written. Dissatisfaction with the level of theory development in comparative research was the direct result of my fieldwork experiences in Japan and Korea from 1969 to 1973, supported by the Fulbright-Hays Fellowship Program. Much of the work reported on here was done during a sabbatical leave granted by the University of Minnesota. A grant from the university Office of International Programs provided travel support to allow the ideas on collective goods to gestate in a proper historical setting; library privileges granted by the London School of Economics are acknowledged. Computer support was provided by the University of Minnesota Computer Center.

I would like to thank James Caporaso, Michael Dellicarpini, William Dunn, George Foster, Timothy Hennessey, Larry Hunter, Robert Kvavik, Craig McCaughrin, Eugene Ogan, John Turner, Patrick Walsh, and Gary Wynia, who read sections of the work. Mitchell Joelson aided in the data analysis. This version of the manuscript will still not satisfy Raymond Duvall. Many points in this essay have been improved as a result of his criticism, and I would like to record my appreciation. In addition, I have worked out some of my ideas in public. For permission to repeat some thoughts here, I am grateful to the editors of *Social Science Quarterly* and Sage Publications and the executive director of the International Studies Association.

1 The Problem

Among advanced industrial or postindustrial societies, as they are called with increasing frequency, there is mounting evidence that something is causing basic changes in the nature of politics itself. No one, to my knowledge, has satisfactorily developed an efficient description, and certainly not an explanation, of this set of changes. However, growing awareness of them is revealed in the rhetoric of politicians, in works by political scientists, and above all in the rise of demands for political participation and of political conflict in several societies. Watergate was a spectacular demonstration of bankruptcy in one central political elite group, a demonstration that has apparently contributed to the decline in citizens' trust of government in the United States; and the fragmentary evidence available for other postindustrial societies suggests a similar decline in public perception of the legitimacy of their political institutions. Villagers along the Franco-German border united to repeal an effort by their respective national governments to place an atomic electrical power plant in their valley. In Japan civic action groups prevented the construction of a new international airport for a decade. In the United States interstate highway construction came to an abrupt halt in the early 1970s as neighborhood action groups became successful in preventing the construction of roads which also led to the destruction of neighborhoods. Attitude surveys in all these and other western European countries show declining public trust in government and growing apathy toward or alienation from the "normal" political institutions such as political parties, and commentators on politics have started writing articles on the demise of party politics and the decline of what are (or were) thought to be high levels of central political institutionalization. The argument that follows is an effort to develop a structuring principle to understand these apparently new types of political participation.

Recent work in the social sciences suggests the presence of a new provisional "pole" in the comparative (cross-national) sociopolitical change process, postindustrialization. My view is that if modernization is captured by the change-to-change metaphor of Huntington (1971), postindustrialization is the phase in which man deals with the implications of that change. If the modernization and industrialization phases of sociopolitical change are directed primarily at growth, postindustrialization is concerned with individual and collective reaction to the slowdown of that growth. Postindustrialization is thus the shift in emphasis from quantitative to qualitative concerns throughout man's social-economic and political activities. It is these assertions that guide my effort in the search for a more systematic description and plausible explanation of postindustrial sociopolitical change.

The argument here departs in two respects from important earlier contributions on the subject of sociopolitical change "beyond development" (see Brzezinski 1970; Hancock and Sjoberg 1972; and Bell 1973). First, I attempt to ground theorizing about such change in empirical data. This portion of the work relies on recent improvements in methods and techniques of comparative research. The specific goal here is to develop a model of social-economic and political change which extends to postindustrialization, a new process-state symbolized by changing ratios in GNP accounted for by the service (including the public) and industrial sectors of the economy. Second, as indicated, the argument seeks to adapt a set of analytics from collective goods theory (sometimes called rational choice, collective action, or social choice) to interpret the suggested model of sociopolitical change.

I hypothesize that mature industrialization is marked by the peaking of industry's share of the economy and the beginning of a shift to the dominance of the service sector, especially public service and regulation. This set of economic changes, combined with other social-economic features, produces the need for structural change in political institutions. The nature of political conflict also changes and follows a sharp rise in political demands that in turn appear to be related to the growing complexity and interdependence of all activities in societies entering the postindustrial phase.

Postindustrialization is also marked by changes in individual values, from an emphasis on the presence of adequate goods, security, and material wants to a primary desire for personal freedom, equality, and justice. I shall attempt to relate this value change to the structural changes in the larger society.

Background: The State of Comparative Research

For a number of years I among others have worked on research problems in comparative politics designed to contribute to the development of a science of comparative political analysis. There has been considerable advancement in the field from the pioneering efforts of Almond and Verba (1963) to the carefully designed comparative studies of Nie, Powell, and Prewitt (1969) and Putnam (1973) of more recent years. However, I think most comparative research specialists would agree that Deutsch's (1963) statement that comparative politics was theory rich but data poor must now be reversed: data of all sorts are relatively more abundant than the theoretical structures so necessary to interpret them. In retrospect, it is understandable that the first comparative research efforts guided by scientific canons of inquiry were directed at data generation and analysis through employment of the computer software routines developed in the late 1950s and early 1960s; and I think it unarguable that there now exists a body of comparative (cross-national) generalizations developed through this work. Comparative politics is now a problem-oriented set of subfields that treat political leadership, participation, and socialization, legislatures, political change, etc., not in geographical isolation but comparatively. Each area program of political research has been enriched by the importation of the comparative frameworks developed by the generalists in the field. The work of specialists has contributed in turn to the conceptual reorganization of the comparative frameworks. However, the goal of a science of comparative research, one in which studies begin to build cumulatively on past work, has not been achieved. Instead, there is a sense of *déjà vu* among those who participated in research and writing during this earlier period. One does not wish to return to the parochial world developed by area specialists, and yet just where do we go from here?

My own answer is that we should rethink our basic assumptions about comparative sociopolitical change and use the analytics of a group of scholars who have developed the collective goods approach which is based on the assumption of individual rational choice. This will allow us to escape the macrosystemic type of thinking that continues to paralyze the field of comparative politics. I wish to examine the utility of working with the methodological assumption of man as a being of rational choice. Starting with this single assumption, I shall attempt to generalize from the individual to collective action groups (including social, economic, and political institutions) in order to discuss problems of government design in postindustrial societies. I have chosen to examine these problems in relation to the rational-choice assumption for a number of reasons. As soon as social scientists move beyond their own society, or even their particular subcultural unit of analysis, the question of the method and techniques of research becomes formidable, indeed often paralyzing to all but the naive or unwary. For example, comparative survey research designs require that linguistic problems be overcome. In a Sapir-Whorfian sense, these difficulties have not and probably will not be overcome. Basic word meanings have an underlying understanding attached to them which is culture-specific. We know, for example, that although the range of refraction of light rays is constant and the range of human ability to perceive this refraction range is also constant, the color continua developed from one culture to the next are not. English has several expressions for what is known simply as "red" in Chinese. The probably bootless search for a culture-free thematic apperception test goes on. The definitions of census data vary considerably from one society to the next, creating interpretation problems. Work in political culture and political socialization teaches us that there are an enormous variety of patterns of social-psychological behavior across nations which we have only begun to examine. The point is that although we should continue to study social-psychological determinants of political behavior, it is time to build upon a common structuring principle, one upon which we can base comparative analysis. We must select a plausible assumption that is capable of allowing the evolution of a body of theory (hypothetico-deductive of politics across nations as well as across systems). The assumption that man is a rational, goal-seeking, value-maximizing or satisficing being is one that escapes social-psychological and cultural bounds on the validity of theory. Giving this assumption *content* does require knowledge of specific cultures, environmental contexts, but this is a basis for theory that is genuinely comparative, i.e., universal.

Synopsis of the Argument

The special claims for a comparative (cross-national) methodology are unwarranted; what unites comparativists is the assumption that there are common processes across systems—as well as within them, across levels, and across time—which warrant examination comparatively. Although in the absence of theory we shall continue to lack any confidence in studies based across as well as within systems, a minimum case for comparative research rests on the notion that the additional variance gained allows checks to be made on within-system studies. A review of methodological and technical problems associated with the study of sociopolitical change suggests specific lessons leading to a process-based methodology for those who would undertake comparative research. Hence an effort is made here to develop an efficient description of a "new" process-state, postindustrialization (with caution from Manheim). To move toward the construction of a (hypothetico-deductive) theory, I develop an argument from collective goods to interpret the political consequences of postindustrialization.

In sum, postindustrialization is marked by the following characteristics: (1) relative increase in the service over the production sector of the economy; (2) slower economic growth, as demand for infrastructure and consumer goods slows; (3) a relative increase in size of the public sector and decline in size of the private sector. From these phenomena follow (4) an assumption that there are upper limits to the public sector and (5) a need for clearer criteria on what should be produced in the public sector and how it should be allocated (from 3 and 4). Because of (1), (2), and (3), there are changing desires in the social sector with respect to institutions and value preferences. (6) Finally, there are important political consequences of all of the foregoing: an increase in nonelectoral political participation, because of the increasingly mixed nature of government goods, and a need for government design alternatives.

Chapter 2 presents the distinctions from the collective goods approach applied to the role of government in sociopolitical change. In the next two chapters I present a model of the political consequences of postindustrialization and an empirical corroboration of its actual presence. Chapters 5-9 assume the argument and (*a*) model the individual value change associated with industrial and postindustrial societies; (*b*) reexamine our concept of development; (*c*) analyze the dominant models, pluralism and corporatism, used in the study of industrial and postindustrial societies; (*d*) present a case study based on a review of local government reform efforts in England; and (*e*) summarize the case for institutional redesign.

The intent of the second part of this book is to develop the implications of the theoretical argument for basic public policy issues in postindustrial societies. However, my purpose is not to provide specific answers to public policy questions but, rather, to inform such discussions with deductions from the theoretical argument presented in chapters 2–4.

Although I have placed my discussion of strategy, methodology, and theory development in comparative research in an appendix, it forms the epistemological underpinnings of the book. Here I present the case for the deductive-theory strategy developed in this book by arguing that debate over the comparative method is actually debate over strategies to achieve better theories in comparative research. What really distinguishes comparative research is its concern with thinking about the social world in terms of movement, change, or process. Thus this argument provides a justification for "discovering" new process-states, such as postindustrialization, in the process of sociopolitical change. Moreover, the appendix justifies the research strategy followed here by evaluating the work done to date in comparative research and sociopolitical change. Debate over fundamental epistemological assumptions is most difficult because of the tacit quality of such assumptions. The argument in the appendix supports my overall purpose, which is to move us away from explanations based on systems and cultures toward those based on individuals.

This book is ultimately based on my personal perception of the main properties and direction of social-economic and political change in postindustrial societies. The model and applications that follow are presented because of my belief in the need to think about such problems, even in the knowledge that such efforts can be only partially successful: broad visions miss much of more specific relevance, and sometimes causes may be inaccurately apprehended. Yet we need to think about the nature of sociopolitical change—and, I might add, in as rigorous a manner as possible—because only by confronting the kinds of questions raised here can we grasp the possible opportunities for redesign that our institutions afford us. If there is merit in my argument that postindustrialization represents a threshold set of societal changes, man once again has significant opportunities to respond creatively and to reorganize the institutions that must deal with the implications of that change.

2 Government and Collective Goods

On the Concept of Goods

Goods are whatever satisfy wants; wants are whatever needs humans perceive as necessary or desirable to fulfill.[1] Wants range from biological requirements—sufficient caloric intake, water, clothing and shelter, and climate supportive of life—to social-psychological desires that include recreation, music, good food, art, etc. Maslow's (1954) value hierarchy indicates how primary wants change; if basic biological wants are satisfied, man is free to attempt to satisfy social-psychological needs. The problem is that once one moves beyond biological wants—and even here it is difficult to know where to draw the line—the question arises as to what determines wants. Economists have long recognized the problems associated with assuming or specifying wants and hence the goods that would satisfy them; positive economics makes no assumptions about the order of the preference schedules of individuals. This has been a useful and wise position that has allowed economists to say a great deal about market, firm, and consumer behavior under idealized conditions. However, the determination, the explanation, of the order of preferences in individual utility schedules has been left to sociologists, anthropologists, psychologists, and indeed all those who attempt to specify the environment within which the individual operates. For obviously it is the nature of the environment—what it provides or denies—that constrains individual determination or wants. This book is really only a series of efforts to show how valuable an exercise it is to link individual choice to environmental conditions which themselves change.

The tacit assumption in all this is one of scarcity. Long ago Robbins defined economics as "the science which studies human behavior as a relationship between ends and scarce means which have alternative uses" ([1932] 1973, p. 16). The point of interest for us, however, is the possibility of extending this assumption to non-market decision-making areas. Specifically, I shall try to sketch a model of government as the provider of certain classes of goods and show how it may be used to interpret sociopolitical change beyond the industrialization process-state.

The Collective Goods Alternative

It is useful to begin by distinguishing the collective goods approach from the other approach taken by political economists, cost-benefit analysis.[2] Both collective goods and cost-benefit analysis employ the language of economists but operate at different levels. Cost-benefit analysis, often called planned program budgeting (PPB) is based on the assumption that rationalization of organizations and institutions is possible; its goal is centralized planning, where sufficient expertise may be assembled to deal with complex policy problems guided by systems analysis. The level of analysis offered is systemic. In comparison, the collective goods approach begins with the methodological assumption of individual rational choice.

We may attach to this simplifying assumption a number of nonobvious aggregation rules about collective action, e.g., the conditions under which individuals will join in group action or comply with leadership desires (see Olson 1965).

However, the heart of the model sketched below rests on a concept of government as the provider of certain classes of goods. In order to define these goods, let us start simply with goods and make the following distinctions. First, the classic definition of private goods is

$$\sum_{i=1}^{\eta} x i = C$$

That is, goods produced for individuals and consumed by them (total consumption C equals the sum of individual consumptions; see table 1). Analytically, pure public goods may be contrasted to private goods; they possess the quality of jointness of supply—their production results in their indivisibility and hence nonexcludibility; if supplied to one member of the community, they cannot be denied to any other member of that community. Examples include national defense, police and fire protection, air pollution control (goods), or inflationary fiscal policies (bads); when provided, all citizens theoretically enjoy their benefits (or liabilities). Hence the opportunity

TABLE 1 **Distinctions between Goods***

	Jointness of Supply	Crowded Supply†	Nonjointness of Supply
Excludible	. . .	Quasi-public (e.g., government subsidies to special groups; pollution from public power plants) Quasi-private (e.g., airlines; communications companies; pollution from private industry)	Private goods (e.g., Reggie Bars, Hondas)
Nonexcludible	Public goods (e.g., national defense; law and order)	. . .	. . .

*All goods in cols. 2 and 3 may be considered collective in nature.
†Goods with significant externalities.

for particular citizens to enjoy benefits without paying their share of the costs (the free rider problem) also exists. The production of many goods results in those that are divisible and thus private. If we produce a Reggie Bar, presumably it may be bought and sold in the marketplace with little argument over its cost; and, more important, there are few or no side effects, i.e., unintended spillover effects (called externalities) attached to the good. However, in between the analytical poles of "pure" public and "pure" private goods are troublesome goods, goods that are called quasi-public or quasi-private or are considered not exclusively private and thus collective in nature. These are crowded in their supply or not purely excludible or nonexcludible. Most observers operate on the assumption that, in any catchment, benefits should exceed costs and that the distribution of benefits and costs should meet the criterion of Pareto optimality (Olson 1969). In fact, pure nonexcludibility is probably impossible. It is very difficult to meet the requirements of the assumption (goal); e.g., in addition to free rider problems, externalities (positive or negative) may induce or prevent attainment of a Pareto-optimal level of production of goods. From the production of goods in factories (private) we receive negative externalities such as pollution. A bread factory may produce negative externalities in the form of traffic congestion because of supply trucks entering and leaving the plant on local roads. The same factory also produces positive externalities in the form of pleasant aromas for adjacent neighbors. From government itself we also may receive such goods as roads that may have unintended negative external effects for the communities adjoining the roads, such as noise and lead pollution and the destruction of existing neighborhoods.

Economists have been reluctant to violate Samuelson's powerful analytical distinctions between public and private goods. In reality there are really very few, if any, goods whose properties allow them to be classified as clearly public or private. I shall argue below that in a postindustrial society it is the rise of collective goods that drives citizens into collective action. There are two closely connected reasons for the rise in collective goods. First, government increasingly provides collective, not public, goods to citizens. Second, citizens in postindustrial societies become more aware of the actual externalities attached to most "private" goods.

These distinctions about goods lead to the following questions:

1. How much is produced—i.e., what is the level of production and consumption?
2. Who allocated the particular scope of inclusiveness (the geographical or functional administrative boundaries)? This question is relevant only if we are concerned with collective (mixed) rather than pure public goods.
3. Who bears the cost?
4. How are the goods produced—i.e., through conscious and concerted collective action or from an externality via other production or consumption activity?

Now if we bring government back into our calculations, we find that much of what it does results in the production and consumption of collective goods.

Politics itself may be defined as conflict—particular questions of social choice and consequent collective action—about the four questions above: political conflict is concerned especially with those nonprivate goods for which government is the provider, either directly as a collective actor or indirectly through externalities from other government action. Moreover, political conflict is concerned with *what* goods will be produced, and *who* decides this as well as who decides questions (1) and (3). If collective goods are increasingly supplanting private and public goods, as I shall argue below, this has fundamental consequences for economics and politics; it suggests the basis for the rebirth of the field of political economy. Collective goods are more divisive and hence conflictual than public or private goods. Where the market operates, citizens presumably match their needs to their resources. And generally the fact that many citizens are free riders on many public goods does not in itself upset citizens because it affects their pocketbooks only marginally. The growing significance of collective goods not only presages a sharp rise in political conflict but also calls into question the structure of government institutions themselves. At the minimum, we must reconsider whether collective goods are most appropriately delivered by centralized political institutions, as compared with public goods.

From modernization through the industrial phase of sociopolitical change, governments concentrate on providing basic or pure public goods, including health and welfare services, when they achieve sufficient resources to do so. However, in what are called postindustrial societies, the increase in government delivery of collective goods results in problems difficult to handle in present government institutions. City-center library services, for example, are consumed by suburban residents who do not pay for their use; those same services may be functionally out of the reach of lower-income groups within the city because of social and economic inequalities reinforced by local government boundaries (R. Hill 1974).

To illustrate how the collective goods approach may be used, let me develop an application in which theory development in comparative research might benefit. The approach is useful for rethinking the centralization principle that underlies virtually all existing models of sociopolitical change, e.g., the steering metaphor of Deutsch (1963), the system perspective of Almond (Almond and Powell 1966), the institutionalization argument of Huntington (1968). These writers share the view that the greater the size of political institutions, the better able they will be to perform their functions.

At the risk of excessive simplification, I group what I consider common positions of these authors and compare them with my own approach. These positions include the view that the political system or central political institutions are the appropriate units of analysis for the study of politics; public interest should take precedence over private interest; fragmentation of political authority is bad and centralization is good. In short, the larger the political unit, the better.

The view that the whole systems approach or holistic versus methodological individualism position is superior is most often based on nothing more than conventional wisdom. After all, most comparative politics specialists are attempting to describe and explain macro features of political change. Elsewhere (Benjamin et al. 1972) I have critically examined the whole systems perspective, and I would only reassert, with Coleman (1972), that the goals of analysts who use the methodological individualism posture include an explanation of collective action units such as groups and institutions.

Affirmation of public over private interest remains fashionable in political science, and especially comparative research. In countries in the modernization phase of change, the laborious process of creating a national political community with an attendant level of public interest means, by definition, the decline of parochial interests of tribal and village communities. As societies move from the industrial to the postindustrial process-state, demands for equality of all citizens begin to take precedence over liberty and efficiency or governmental effectiveness. This brings the question of a generalized social welfare—one in the public interest—to the head of the national political agenda and, again, would appear to warrant a national—centralized—solution. However, from Arrow (1951) we know the impossibility of such welfare functions. This fact has significance for all those attempting to contribute to the public/private interest debate; it does not mean, though, that we must retreat to a nineteenth-century liberalism view that denies the claims of all groups. It does mean that we should think very carefully about all claims put forth as being in the public interest (M. Taylor 1976). The assumption used by most writers is that fragmentation of political units is bad and centralization is good. In addition to the points raised below concerning efficiency and the need to differentiate among public goods and the size of government units appropriate to deliver them, there are questions of coordination, equality of services, and the complexity of government itself. The assertion is questionable that greater hierarchy of control is preferable because it presumably wipes out the uncoordinated and inefficient provision of public goods associated with decentralized government units and their overlapping jurisdictions and functions. In fact there are numerous theoretical and empirical studies that provide support for nonhierarchical bargaining coordination in the public sector.

With respect to the problem of delivery of goods, there are two points. Proponents of widening the catchment to provide more equal distribution assume that all individuals have identical tastes and/or incomes and therefore desire the same mix of public goods. This assumption is rarely borne out. Second, one may simply assume that everyone should in principle consume the same amount of public goods; this is also inappropriate. Where government action is necessary to ensure minimum provision of public goods, legislative action by a higher political unit may be taken to provide it. The point to remember is that creation of large catchments may widen inequalities rather than narrow them. Finally, complexity itself is adjudged sufficient reason to move to larger units. For example, in local government many observers argue that excessive numbers of political units in metropolitan areas mean that the individual citizen may not be able to keep track of them. However, one may assert with equal plausibility that the larger the unit of political control, the less it will be responsive to individual claims. At bottom rest the positive images evoked by centralization and the negative images suggested by decentralization. Surely it is not inappropriate at least to question the assumptions behind these images and offer an alternative. I shall translate a portion of the discussion about centralization into the relationship between size and efficiency.

Size and efficiency. Greater size has been assumed to lead to the achievement of a "critical mass," defined as an organization sufficiently large to allow the necessary specialization to perform competently the function relevant to its organizational goals. It has also been felt that greater size promotes economies of scale. However, the collective goods approach suggests a view of the effects of size on efficiency that alerts us to the possibility that the greater the size, the lower the level of efficiency (Tullock 1965; Downs 1967).

Bureaucratic organizations may be perceived as structures staffed by self-interested individuals. In theory, advancement in the organization comes to those who perform assigned tasks most successfully; in fact, however, rewards are most likely to go to those who perform functions in a manner most congruent with the organization's latent goals. These include selection of such problem solutions that will preclude risking failure and, most important, the transfer of information which inferiors feel their superiors want to hear. Information about bureaucratic failure or a problem that must be solved is unwelcome, because it requires action that may have uncertain consequences for the superior. All of this results in information bias; the more levels through which information passes, the greater the possibility that the information will be biased. Furthermore, the same information bias occurs between departments competing for funds, power, and advantage within the larger organization. When we look at the relationship between size and efficiency from the collective goods approach, we should therefore be prepared to find diseconomies as well as economies of scale.[3]

The need to differentiate among public goods. A return to the public/private goods distinction and the discussion of collective goods suggests a different view concerning the question of the government organization to be considered appropriate for the delivery of different types of public goods. Although research is only beginning on the implications of the nature of public goods for the optimum size and type of government units, several points are clear. Where services are more rather than less sensitive to information (requiring more rather than fewer sender-receiver interactions), smaller, not larger, government units are to be preferred. For example, while the errors associated with the information transfers dealing with the problem of sewage disposal may not be large, this is not likely to be the case with education or social, health, or welfare services. In addition, free rider problems tend to arise where there is confusion over who is to pay for services or where there are few negative sanctions or positive incentives for the individual to pay. This can mean, as appears to be the case with the National Health Service in postindustrial Britain, that underinvestment in capitalization occurs, coupled with overutilization of the service since it is "free." This results in a health service shored up financially by the central government only sporadically. Alternatively, small government units may create islands of privilege by developing high-quality services for their clients while excluding nonresidents from using those services, even though they may be paying for them through taxes. It may also be the case that nonresidents gain significant free rider benefits by being able to enjoy the benefits of neighborhood parks, concerts, and other locally provided programs without paying their share of the costs that fall on residents of the authority. Finally, the need for many specific types of social services is sporadic. For instance, the need for health care and police organizations large enough to support specialists able to handle any contingency is cited as an argument for centralization in postindustrial societies. But what do the riot squads or special kidney transplant teams do when they are not being used? Often small government units operating with part-time or volunteer support provide more flexible and less costly service (Ostrom, Parks, and Whitaker 1973). Perhaps too much specialization, too well organized, is too much of a good thing after all.[4] Should one be surprised by research findings of diseconomies of scale related to increased size of government units? Not from the collective goods approach; it seems, rather, that economies of scale may be achieved when dealing with more mechanized services such as air pollution control, transportation networks, etc.; while diseconomies of scale and U-shaped curves flow from other services. This should alert us to the need to differentiate among public goods.

Implications

In the collective goods approach we may visualize a continuum of goods from private to public. For all but a very few private goods the approach reaffirms the fact that most decisions have *joint* political-economic determinants and consequences. The approach places the focus on the need to construct typologies of goods that are most significant at different points in the sociopolitical change process. Whether public-private or public-collective-private mixes of goods predominate in society has fundamental consequences for (*a*) the nature and level of political conflict and (*b*) the system of institutional design appropriate to respond to the society's particular mix of goods. If there are substantial disjunctions between political institutions and the goods they are delivering, e.g., the point of size/differentiation of goods, there will be substantial political problems. Finally, the collective goods approach places the individual squarely at the center of decision making and allows us to exploit the explanatory power of the hypothetico-deductive models that have served economics so well.

Let us turn next to a sketch of postindustrialization and suggest basic political consequences from the collective goods model.

3 The Political Consequences of Postindustrialization

The utility of the collective goods approach becomes clear when we sketch a model that departs from recent work relevant to comparative sociopolitical change. Although in principle the model is applicable to process-states other than postindustrialization, I shall concentrate on those variables which I believe are producing the structural change from industrialization to postindustrialization. I reiterate that my goal concerns the identification of the salient descriptive characteristics of the postindustrial process-state; no unidirectional change throughout all existing societies is assumed.

The terms "modernization," "industrialization," and "postindustrialization" are used in this study in a descriptive sense rather than as concepts which have intrinsic meaning in themselves. The terms are meant to identify different process-states in sociopolitical change with corresponding different first-order constellations of problems. I am not here concerned with what causes modernization, industrialization, or postindustrialization.[1] I do assume the contents of an efficient description of postindustrialization to have fundamental implications for the political process.

Models of modernity conceived during the 1950s and 1960s now form an inappropriate polarity that blinds students to the prospect, the reality, of further change. This problem appears to be caused by ignorance of new threshold points in the socioeconomic process of change that have important political consequences. The onset of postindustrialization, as stated, is marked by a decline in the rate of increase of the industrial sector of the economy and a rise in the rate of increase of the service sector, especially public and regulatory. A number of studies have described the properties of each of these dimensions (Brzezinski 1970; Inglehart 1971; and especially Bell 1973), but in my judgment it is in the reaction to the slowdown of the rate of change and the nature of that change that the new provisional benchmark for the sociopolitical change process develops. I shall limit discussion to the main points of interest. Figure 1 summarizes the model by presenting a family of curves that indicate the direction of change in politically relevant areas; what follows are the assertions of the argument.

A key element in my model is the shift to the dominance of the service sector. Postindustrialization also comprises changing social needs and corresponding changing emphases in social institutions. A decline in birth rates and an increase in longevity create new problems for the education, health, and the overall economic system. Schools go empty, people not only live longer—to the point where a virtually new generation is emerging—but have increased expectations about the quality of health care and the quality of their social and economic lives as well. Moreover, in addition to value changes (Inglehart 1971, 1977*b*), postindustrialization loosens institutionalized parameters, such as family and community, that formerly provided boundaries for individual choice. In the political

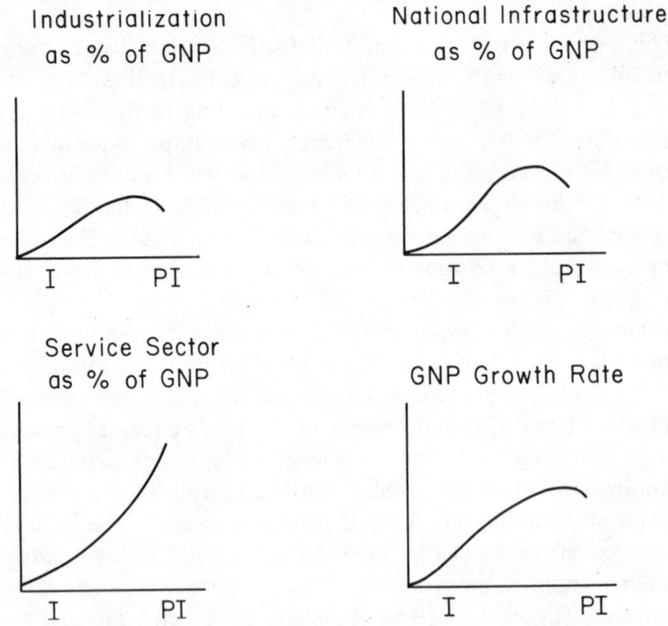

Fig. 1. Industrialization (I) and postindustrialization (PI): some definitional characteristics.

arena, postindustrialization involves a sharp rise in demands for participation and a rise in local community action groups, which perhaps contribute to the decline in political party identification and growth of apathy toward existing political institutions. It is also the period in which crises in planning and bureaucratic decision making become especially significant. However, let us turn to the specific hypotheses in the economy, social areas, and political arena.

The economy. Whereas the main assumption behind industrialization is growth in terms of developing the infrastructure of the economy—e.g., transportation, power, and communication networks, as well as the capital (or the framework within which to get it) necessary to generate in turn self-generating industrial development—the driving assumption in the postindustrialization phase is the need to deal with the implications of this economic growth. This point reflects the fact that when most consumers have durable goods sufficient to their material needs, their demand and hence the rate of increase in production of those goods declines and reaches equilibrium. At some point in economic development focus begins to shift from development to maintenance of the basic goods supplied by government. Some popular writers have attempted to capture aspects of this change process in the "limits of growth" metaphor. Surely one may expect a finite number of railroads, highways, or telephones in a society; perhaps our previous obsession with growth and development blinded us to this fact. Postindustrialization follows this peak point, as illustrated in figure 2.

The changeover to the new process-state has several consequences. The service sector begins to grow—slowly at first, then with increasing speed—until it becomes the largest share of the economy.[2] The nature of the economy shifts from the production of goods to the production of services. This may indeed mean the growing ascendancy of the codification of knowledge (defined in research and development terms) and its products becoming the dominant feature of society (Bell 1973). Many societies, however, lack sufficient human and financial resources to mount credible research and development programs; for these, employment will more probably rise in satellites of large multinational firms, service-related industries, and the public sector. Partly as a consequence of this structural change in the nature of the economy, the rate of economic growth, as traditionally measured by economists (i.e., the rate of increase in GNP), declines.

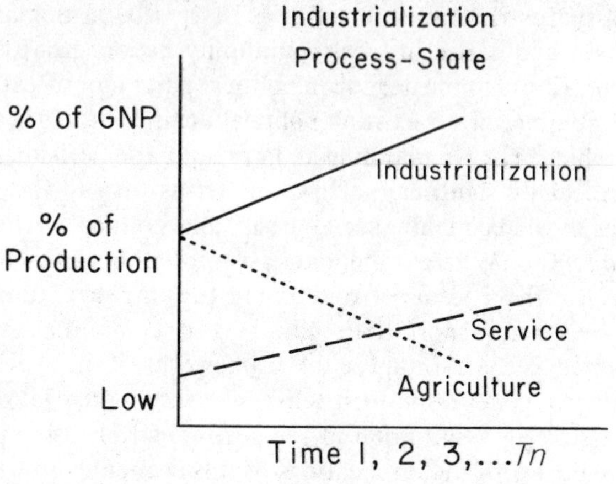

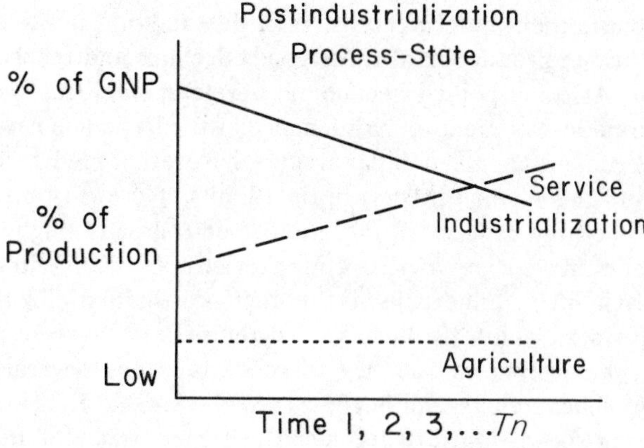

Fig. 2

The concept of the service sector itself needs more attention than I can give it here. First, much work needs to be done on what the concept comprises and what impact it has on the economy. The general assumption is that service activities make inferior contributions to the GNP as compared with industry. Yet the burgeoning services in postindustrial societies, both private and public, clearly do improve our lives in innumerable ways. Many private service companies are available to facilitate citizens' ability to satisfy their wants, e.g., to improve their housing, to travel, to enjoy social and cultural activities. In fact improvement of the service sector is central to the development of better information systems that become an economic need in postindustrial society. Second, although I think it reasonable to expect the eventual slowdown of energy production and consumption, for reasons similar to those just given, its production and consumption will rise for a considerable period in postindustrial societies as a function of the accelerated development and use of specialized technologies and the continued increase in material comforts in the home and office.

There is also a clear overall decline in the proportion of the work force in the postindustrial production sector. This is because of a *relative* decline in the need for blue-collar workers resulting from the stabilization of the need for infrastructure goods. Yet this raises fundamental distribution questions. Income inequality increases during the process of change associated with industrialization (*Royal Commission on the Distribution of Income and Wealth* 1975). The problems generated by this fact, generally grouped under the relative-deprivation hypothesis, may or may not be solved by the time the country enters the postindustrial process-state; if they are not, successive layers of stratification may combine to confront the central political institutions with more severe problems. New cleavages may simply be added to the old, but possibilities for new coalitions may form as well. For example, black and white blue-collar workers may form a new coalition against the white suburban white-collar interests. Public and private white-collar interests may compete for scarce resources in the face of a declining tax base, and yet I know of no formula that will eliminate the rising inequalities that appear to be part of earlier modernizing and industrializing process-states.

With no offsetting supply and demand constraints, as in the market economy, the fiscal demands of the state have no particular limits beyond those forced upon them by government structures. This situation creates what Brittan (1975) calls the economic contradictions of a liberal democracy, because it essentially is a common-pool problem; even if everyone recognizes the merit of halting raids on the public treasury, which may have declining resources, it is never in the interests of particular labor unions or other organized interest groups to limit their demands, for they have no guarantee that others will do the same. Inflation creates internal conditions that compel the leaders of interest groups to make such demands.

The point is simply what I take to be a fundamental economic dilemma in postindustrial societies. Citizen wants may be as high as before; the inequalities left over from earlier periods of change may require substantial economic redress; and yet changes in the basic structure of the economy indicate a slowdown in the rate of growth. In fact a scaling down of the desire for material goods appears desirable or even necessary. One reason this may occur is due to the implications I project concerning the range of the salary structure in postindustrial society, which is increasingly dominated by public activists. The criteria used for efficiency and increase in productivity remain quantitatively oriented; a plant produces more automobiles at lower cost; this is prima facie evidence of the organization's increased productivity and efficiency. However, if we visualize a continuum of human activity with the private goods at one end and public goods at the other, the usual productivity criteria become less relevant as we approach the public goods end. Throughout the range of production and consumption of goods and services such as police protection, welfare, and education, it is clear, I think, that new performance measures must be devised. For example, is the policeman who arrests more people more "productive" than his colleague who arrests fewer but engages in crime-prevention activity? Is a professor who turns out more or fewer students, ten or five papers each year, more efficient and "productive?" In fact, of course, less rather than more may mean better, especially in human services where intensive individual contact is required. This is important because in my argument postindustrialization is marked by a slowdown in economic growth. In discussing the public and private sectors of the economy, Baumol puts the argument slightly differently:

> Economic activity can be divided into two types: technical progressive activity in which innovation, capital accumulation, and economies of large scale all make for a cumulative rise in output per man-hour and activities which, by their very nature, permit only sporadic increases in productivity. If productivity per man-hour rises cumulatively in one sector relative to its rate of growth elsewhere in the economy, while wages rise commensurately in all areas, then relative costs in the non-progressive sectors must inevitably rise, and these costs will rise cumulatively and *without limit.* [Baumol 1969, p. 109; emphasis added]

To the extent that conditions meeting Baumol's requirements develop, the public sector will necessarily undergo substantial alteration. The question concerns the upper limit of this sector's proportion of the GNP. For the public sector (which in Baumol's terms is nonprogressive, and hence one in which relative costs will inevitably rise), this means that, over time, for the same dollars one purchases fewer and fewer relative services, which brings on the real upper limits more rapidly. Nowhere is there evidence that the public's demands are satiated—government burdens continue to grow (King 1975), and yet there appear to be upper limits that are being reached in poorer members of the postindustrial group, such as Britain (Lapping 1970).

Social change. My assumption is that social change follows the economic change described above. Values and attitudes may be defined as individual cognitive orientations conceived of as preference schedules that change in regular and predictable fashion when shifts occur in the social-economic environment (see chaps. 5 and 6). First, I shall sketch the social concomitants of the economic change process.

Ecologically, there comes a point when the rate of increase in urbanization declines and the flight to the suburbs begins. One reason for this change concerns the new set of spatial and communication possibilities afforded by the articulation of complex transportation networks and equally complex and sophisticated information systems that accompany the development of postindustrialization. Whereas in the industrial process-state urban centers appear necessary for economic activity, this may no longer be entirely the case in postindustrial societies, because urban centers serve to solve the nonstandardization substitution problems of industrial plants. In the production of goods, "down time" results in loss of man hours and hence money; service personnel in satellite industries and the work force for the factory itself must be close by. If development in transportation and communication networks means that close proximity is no longer required, the need for urban solutions to economic problems is no longer pressing. Postindustrial cities will have to be based on social and cultural requirements in the future (see chap. 7).

It is also interesting to note changes in communications and other areas. If we translate tables into graphs, general mass communication systems are constructed, peak, and then make way for increasingly specialized communication needs of better educated and more differentiated publics (Maisel 1973; Inglehart 1971). The same kind of shift of concern from basic institutions designed to deliver basic goods to the quality of performance occurs elsewhere. For example, once educational systems are established throughout society, concern turns to consideration of their quality of performance. Should we be surprised at this? I think not, if we link the recent reports of value change in postindustrial societies, e.g., Britain, the Scandinavian countries, Japan (Marsh 1975; Kvavik 1976; Ike 1973) to the discussion presented here. The reported changes concern the apparent shift in values from a high priority for economic security, order, and authority to an emphasis on notions of freedom and social justice. I hypothesize that these value changes (preference-schedule orderings in individual utility schedules) are individual responses to fundamental changes in the social-economic environment. If the content of preference schedules is a function of individuals' cognitive orientation toward their environment, once wants associated with economic needs are satisfied, attention turns to preferences associated with postindustrialization, preferences formerly subordinated. This basic change in the cognitive orientation of individuals supports the shift in public concern from the existence of services and economic sufficiency to the quality of these services (see chap. 5).

Political change. All of the foregoing is prefatory to a sketch of the political consequences of postindustrialization. To put it forcefully, existing political structures in postindustrial societies were designed to meet the needs of modernizing and industrializing societies, not the requirements of citizens in postindustrial societies. The main problem has to do with the structural arrangements developed to handle political conflict in industrial societies. Emphasis during the period of industrialization is on the growth of government. During this period elites and scholars develop the argument that in size rests efficiency, and hence, as institutions eventually become centralized, one might expect the decline of politics or at least of polarized conflict. However, if my hypothesis of the shift of emphasis from growth and development to quality is accurate, size per se may not be a virtue. The reasons for this rest in my collective goods argument about the implications of postindustrialization for politics.

Although there has been a return by some to the "end of ideology" scenario attached to some postindustrial discussions (Bell 1973), other writers have begun to describe the political implications of postindustrialization more accurately. These include the change to the dominance of participation over authority, the decline in acceptance of the legitimacy of basic existing political institutions, and the development of new polarizations of private and public white-collar groups, and blue and white-collar groups (Huntington 1974). One also finds that discussion may emerge of other types of conflict, such as revolution redefined (McCaughrin 1976).

However, a number of additional implications follow from the sketch of social-economic change presented here. A basic question concerning welfare services in postindustrial societies is, How much is enough? For instance, consider health care, whose continued development would appear noncontroversial. Yet in Sweden, a country with perhaps the longest record concerning the development of health care systems, the question of the relative benefits of additional expenditures is being debated. If Baumol (1967) is correct and the shift to the public sector is an accurate characterization, economic imperatives will force a reordering of public priorities. Already in some societies such as Britain, where there has been a rapid shift to the service (including the public) sector, but without the development of a partially offsetting research and development sector, the financial burdens of the public are becoming too difficult to bear.

Additionally, there are a host of interstate questions concerning the problems of economic, political, and even military conflict which exist between postindustrial societies and industrial and modernizing systems (Huntington 1974). Can postindustrial societies, in which public preference schedule changes may make the continuance of industry difficult, compete with industrializing countries? That is, can postindustrial societies maintain an industry sector to support their large public sectors? Can these societies raise large conventional armies, which by definition are incongruent with dominant cognitive orientations emphasizing individual values of self-expression and freedom?

Moreover, the evolution of the postindustrial process-state also may involve the decline of the grip of nationalism on citizens—which grows as societies modernize. The growth of nationalization is congruent with the construction of the national infrastructure, the growth of a larger shared set of norms and values—beyond the villages and the region, etc. Some observers see nation building as a prerequisite to modernization itself. Moreover, a perpetual lament of smaller western European industrialized states is that they do not possess the population necessary to allow the economies of scale that manufacturers in the United States enjoy. Indeed, as societies modernize, whether socialist, capitalist, or communist, the state offers its citizens an ideology that is essentially a political religion. In postindustrial societies nationalism—a process of individual psychological identification with a particular, usually spatially limited reference unit—begins to weaken in the face of both supra- and subnational claims of authority or autonomy. Reasons for this change may be investigated in at least three areas. First, most postindustrial societies contain minority groups that—like working-class elements—have not shared equally in economic development during the industrialization process; for these groups economic and social inequality may also remain constant. If, as is often the case, the deprived group is distinguished by ethnic, geographical, linguistic, and possibly religious characteristics that isolate them from the mainstream, it is natural for this group to reassert itself as a vigorous collective action unit when (*a*) the promises of the dominant group(s) in society grow hollow and (*b*) the disadvantaged group realizes that strong sanctions (e.g., by the police or the military) are improbable. Examples include the Welsh and Scots in Britain; the Basques, Catalans, and Bretons in Spain and France; the French in Canada. This trend may be expected to increase as other societies move into the postindustrial phase. Moreover, the legitimacy of ethnic group claims may rise during other phases of sociopolitical change because of the impact of the achievement of ethnic groups in postindustrial societies. Third, the growth in interdependence is not confined to within-system (one-country) activities. The inability of nation-states as collective action units to meet the challenge of international system-generated negative externalities—from water or air pollution, migration, economic behavior of multinational corporations—is well documented. The growth of collective goods in the international system accompanies the growth in global interdependence and the decline of sovereignty in all nation-states. Effective collective action in the face of many problems in the international system will come only from supranational collective action units. Thus examples like the European Economic Community, the United Nations (at least portions of it) the International Monetary Fund, the World Bank, and the Law of the Seas Conference will proliferate. Finally, if the argument that value change accompanies postindustrialization is accurate, it is reasonable to expect a diminution of unquestioning attachment and obedience to the nation-state itself. Several mixes of incentives and sanctions will encourage this change. Economic interdependence across societies brings the eventual recognition of a fate common to all humans. International travel and communication are greater for citizens of postindustrial societies than for inhabitants of industrial societies; this may also reduce the citizen's concept of people from other societies as the faceless "other."

Debates over fragmentation within nations—the rise of subnational groups—and the supplanting of the nation-state by supranational units continue in isolation from each other. This is perhaps another example of how we remain prisoners of political designs articulated in earlier periods of sociopolitical change. There is no a priori reason not to experiment with designs of political authority. There is no compelling reason why all aspects of sovereignty over the affairs of citizens should reside in one unit. Citizens of EEC countries such as Britain may soon come to exchange local representatives among their devolved assemblies, e.g., in Scotland, Wales, and England, and sent them to Brussels itself. The point is that the focus of political conflict around the design of units of sovereignty is changing in postindustrial societies.

The Inferences

The questions to be answered, then, are as follows: (1) How and why does the rise in the demand for public (collective) goods occur? (2) Why do different public (collective) goods imply different efficiency criteria, and why do these criteria imply different size principles?

First, the fact that postindustrial society is interdependent (LaPorte 1975) has an independent effect that aids the rise of political conflict. "Interdependence," in the analytic language used here, is a summary term indicating the growth of externalities, positive and negative, throughout society. If in fact economic systems and their subsystems become dependent on one another for their existence, mutual concern for the other's activities rises. In addition, interdependence is facilitated by the greater ease—through better communication and transportation networks—with which citizens may satisfy wants, wants which are themselves now differentiated. In turn this means that there is an increasing necessity for individuals to control access to themselves. We may point to two additional reasons why demands for collective goods rise. Changes in values and public educational and material resource levels surely have a good deal to do with it. When man is concerned with securing basic levels of food, clothing, and shelter, he is less likely to be worried about ecological issues. Once adequate material conditions for existence are developed, he has time to think about the actual externalities attached to goods thought previously to be private in nature, e.g., the current effort to regulate smoking. In fact one of the major issues in postindustrial societies is likely to be that of drawing the line between collective and private goods. The interaction between citizens and government points to the second additional cause of the increase. It cannot be surprising that once government provides the more nearly "pure" type of public goods described above, government and public attention turns to more specific goods. Not only are there career-related incentives for bureaucratic elites to extend the service they deliver, but the public they serve is increasingly differentiated and begins to request, for example, specific kinds of educational aid for handicapped children, not just support for education itself. Moreover, the increase in collective goods—originating from public or private sources—creates a bandwagon effect. The individual citizen is driven to government, including the courts, either to counteract the local park board's new scheme to enlarge the park, which has the incidental effect of reducing his front yard, or to try to get the park board to adopt a different scheme for the park. Finally, government provision of goods previously provided by the private sector lessens the survivability of the nongovernment institutions. Is it really so surprising that growth in government expenditures on higher education has coincided with the decline of private colleges and universities? For all but the wealthiest institutions, the outlook is bleak if one expects only private support to carry them, because there is little incentive for most citizens to contribute; they already pay taxes, and a reasonable standard of education is provided by public institutions. And the cost of interdependence and increase in demands for government delivery of quasi-public goods (subcategories of collective goods) create problems because "diverse wants or values with respect to collective goods are a basis for conflict, whereas different wants with respect to individual or private goods are not. . . . Everyone in the domain of a given collective good must put up with about the same level and type of collective good, whereas with different tastes for private goods each individual can consume whatever mix of goods he prefers" (Olson 1965, p. 173).

Equally important is the fact that in postindustrial societies the need arises to develop efficiency criteria to deal with economies and diseconomies of scale. Perhaps during the growth periods of modernization and industrialization large-scale government institutions were sufficient for the purpose of laying down the national infrastructure. However, the postindustrial period brings a necessity for innovation in the design of government institutions.[3] This is essentially a question of the optimal distribution of collective or quasi-public goods provided by government—a problem which receives little attention in modernizing or industrializing societies. Even if one accepts standard cost/benefit calculations as efficiency criteria, greater size does not lead inevitably to the achievement of economies of scale. Definitions of economies and diseconomies of scale usually relate to the degree of efficiency of production that in turn is measured by cost/benefit factors. For example, "more efficient use of resources means that total output increases with the same inputs. Increases in productivity are the result both of increased physical capital and of improved technology" (Pechman 1975, p. 33). Not only are economies of scale often not achieved in distribution of goods by government units of greater size, but other distributional criteria such as equity are not included in such standard definitions of economies of scale.[4]

In the collective goods approach, neither centralization of government nor total decentralization to the local level appears appropriate. What is called for is a recognition of the need for flexible government organizational responses to increasingly differentiated public- and collective-good needs. Some services like water, pollution control, or defense may be optimally provided by large-scale government units. Others, which deal with information-sensitive problems of quality control, may be more appropriately provided by smaller units of government.

4 Empirical Correlates of the Postindustrial Process-State

The foregoing discussion remains conjecture without empirical corroboration. I note the provisional nature of the exercise; much work must be devoted to data collection before we reach a satisfactory point in an empirical analysis of the postindustrial process.

At the outset let me summarize the principles governing the analysis. First, the goal is to make point predictions about the strength as well as the direction of relationships. It is also important to view relationships in the process sense discussed in the appendix; this means giving attention to rates of change and cross-time as well as cross-sectional comparisons. The analysis itself will be devoted simply to substantiating the presence of the postindustrial process-state.

The unit of analysis is the nation-state, although I reiterate the importance of within-system, regional, and cross-level variation.

To begin with, I present four graphs of representative measures of the industrial and service shares (especially including the government) of the GNP over selected cross-time comparisons for Denmark, Sweden, Britain, and the United States (see figs. 3–6). Although the rate at which emphasis changes from industry to the service sector differs across societies, and within each of them across time, the shape and direction of the curves corroborate the projections presented in figure 1. Britain appears to have gone farthest in changeover; there the public sector alone accounts for a greater share of the GNP than the manufacturing sector.

Next, I attempt a macro-level comparison with a data set of sixty-four countries that were selected on the basis of data availability and range of variation; all that was necessary was the presence of an array of countries sufficient to allow testing of the presence or absence of properties defined as postindustrial. In other words, I wish to test whether one can distinguish a group of countries with postindustrial versus industrial characteristics.

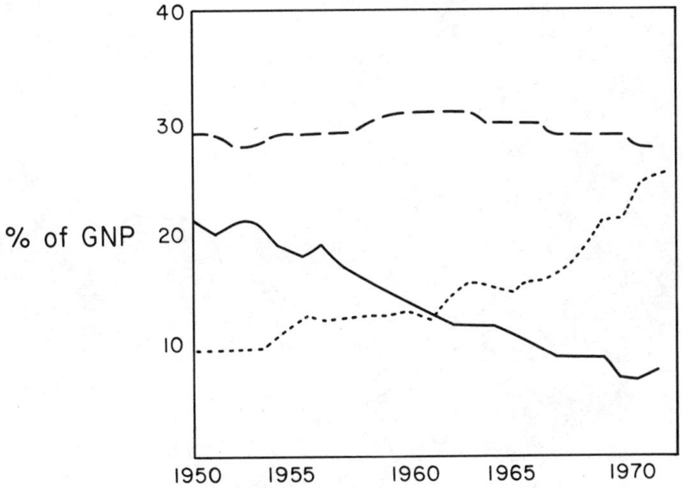

Fig. 3. GNP by sectoral origin: Denmark, 1950–73. Solid line: GNP by agriculture; broken line: GNP by industry; dotted line: GNP by government sector.

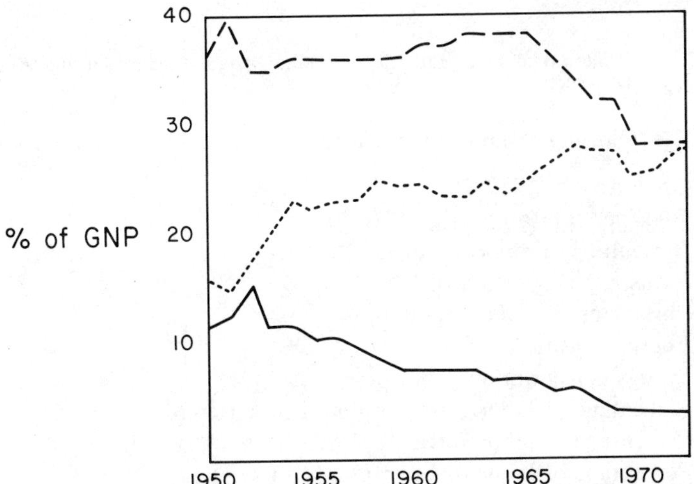

Fig. 4. GNP by sectoral origin: Sweden, 1950–73. See legend to fig. 3

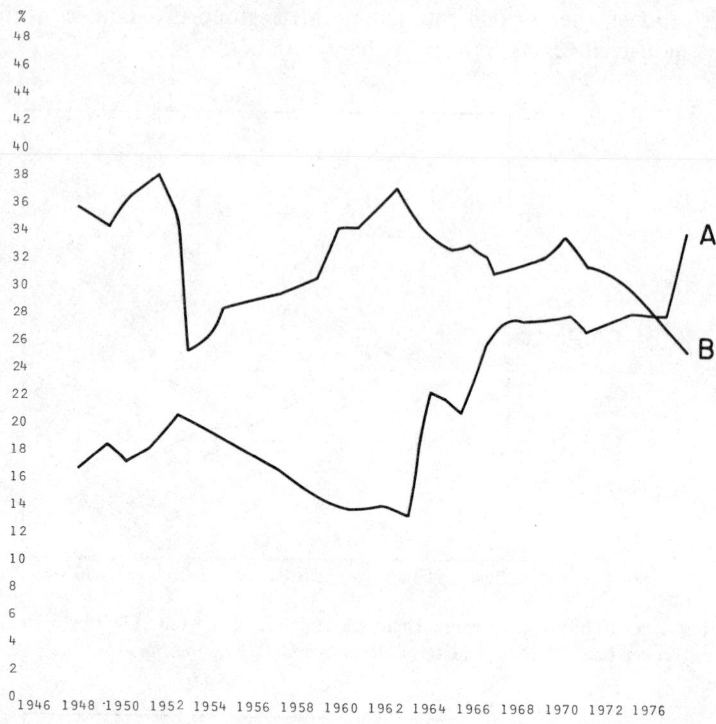

Fig. 5. Britain: total public authority expenditure (*A*) and manufacturing (*B*) as percentages of GNP.

The following social-economic measures were used in the analysis:

GNP growth, 1960–70
GNP per capita growth, 1960–70
Agricultural proportion of GNP
Industrial proportion of GNP
Physicians per 1,000 population
Energy consumption
Energy consumption per capita
Percentage of labor force employed in agriculture
Percentage of labor force employed in industry
Percentage of labor force employed in services

Most of the measures are familiar and do not require extensive justification in and of themselves; what is important is how they are

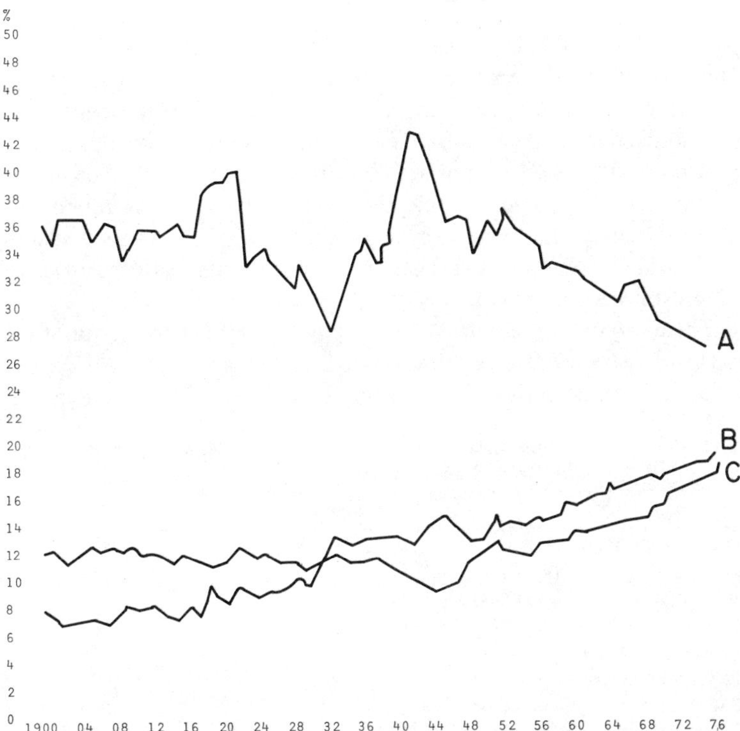

Fig. 6. United States: percentage of employment in manufacturing (*A*), government (*B*), and services (*C*).

seen to fit the appropriate defining characteristics of the postindustrial process-state. Gross national product is a base measure for the first two measures, gross national product growth and gross national product per capita growth, calculated for 1960–70. The hypothesis is that postindustrial societies should exhibit slower growth rates during this period than industrializing countries. Both agricultural and industrial proportions of the GNP should be lower in postindustrial societies. Due to data limitations, I was unable to develop a summary measure appropriate for the service sector of the society. However, one example that taps service dimensions is the number of physicians per 1,000 population. Here as elsewhere, it will be important to expand the number of indicators. Health concerns in postindustrial societies may be at significantly higher levels than in industrializing societies—thus the health variable should score higher when I undertake a factor analysis in the former group. The percentages of the labor force employed in agriculture, industry, and services measure whether industry or the service sector of the economy is dominant. Finally, although I expect energy consumption and energy consumption per capita eventually to decline in postindustrial, as compared with industrial, societies, the consumer demands of the larger middle class plus start-up costs related to information-system technology in the service sector suggest that it is reasonable to hypothesize higher energy requirements in countries in the postindustrial group.

The analysis and results. Since it is reasonable to assume that many of the variables are interrelated, factor analysis is an appropriate technique with which to infer the presence or absence of the

TABLE 2 **Postindustrialization Dimensions Factor Matrix (after Rotation with Kaiser Normalization)**

	Postindustrialization	Industrialization
GNP growth, 1960-70	.272	.895
GNP per capita growth, 1960-70	-.171	.828
Agricultural proportion of GNP	-.821	-.094
Industrial proportion of GNP	.168	.960
Physicians per 1,000 population	.388	-.006
Labor force employed in agriculture (%)	-.130	-.002
Labor force employed in industry (%)	-.825	-.015
Labor force employed in services (%)	.898	.221
Energy consumption	.931	-.149
Energy consumption per capita	.111	-.226

SOURCES. GNP per capita growth: *United Nations Statistical Yearbook* (New York: U.N. Department of Economic and Social Affairs Statistical Office, 1974), pp. 634-38. Agricultural and industrial proportions of GNP: ibid., pp. 622-34. Physicians per 1,000,000 population: ibid., pp. 781-86. Students in post-secondary enrollment: ibid., pp. 820-45. Labor force in agriculture, industry, and services: International Labour Office, *Yearbook of Labour Statistics* (Geneva: ILO, 1974), pp. 737-53. Energy consumption and energy consumption per capita: *United Nations Statistical Yearbook*, pp. 359-63. Government budgets: ibid., pp. 682-771. U.S. GNP: U.S. Bureau of the Census, *Historical Statistics* (Washington, D.C.: Government Printing Office, 1970), pp. 131-45; and Michael Hudson and Charles Taylor, *World Handbook of Social and Political Indicators. II* (New Haven: Yale University Press, 1972). British GNP: Great Britain, Central Statistical Office, *Annual Abstract of Statistics* (London: Her Majesty's Stationery Office, 1975), pp. 327-45. Swedish and Danish GNP: B. R. Mitchell, *European Historical Statistics* (New York: Columbia University Press, 1975), pp. 697-706.

postindustrial condition. Rao's canonical factor analysis technique is used with appropriate assumptions.[1] First, factor analysis using the foregoing variables was undertaken to ascertain whether the postindustrial process-state can be distinguished from the industrial one. Table 2 presents the principal results of the factor analysis extracted after rotation with the Kaiser normalization criterion. The direction and specific strength of the Pearson *R* coefficients reported do distinguish the two process-states, and generally in the manner expected. In fact the distinctions drawn are striking: at least in terms of these measures, there is "development" beyond industrialization. To validate further the factors distinguished in table 2, I computed a small-space analysis of the variables used in the analysis; the results (fig. 7), based on metric assumptions, corroborate the original findings presented in table 2. Table 3 presents the countries, factor scores, and cut-off points used to establish the

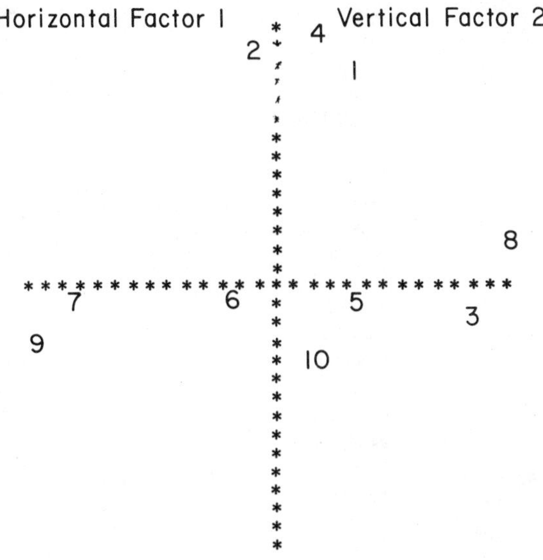

Fig. 7. Factors of postindustrial development. Horizontal factor 1: postindustrialization; vertical factor 2: industrialization. 1: GNP growth, 1960–70; 2: GNP per capita growth, 1960–70; 3: agricultural proportion of GNP; 4: industrial proportion of GNP; 5: health (physicians per 1,000 population); 6: energy consumption; 7: per capita energy consumption; 8: labor force percentage in agriculture; 9: labor force percentage in industry; 10: labor force percentage in services. Factors 3–10 for 1970.

TABLE 3 Countries, Factor Scores, and Cut-off Points Used to Establish Postindustrialization and Industrialization

Category	Country	Postindustrialization Factor Score
Postindustrial	Belgium	-1.69
	Denmark	-1.59
	Czechoslovakia	-1.49
	Norway	-1.40
	Britain	-1.24
	Sweden	-1.19
	West Germany	-1.16
	Netherlands	- .94
	Switzerland	- .89
	Canada	- .77
	East Germany	- .72
	Austria	- .69
	France	- .66
	United States	- .50
Industrial	Rumania	- .41
	Argentina	- .27
	Bulgaria	- .25
	Chile	- .16
	South Africa	- .09
	Spain	- .03
	Mexico	.04
	Brazil	.26
	Colombia	.34
	Burma	.46
	Morocco	.59
	Turkey	.67
	Albania	.90
	Pakistan	1.21
	India	1.31
	Guatemala	1.35
	Philippines	1.55
	Venezuela	1.56
	Kenya	1.69
	Peru	1.82
	Thailand	2.15
	South Korea	2.29

NOTE. Mean = .017; maximum = 1.690; maximum = 2.290. A basic reason why countries like the United States and France rank low in the postindustrial category is that they also load positively on variables associated with industrialization, such as the agricultural proportion of the GNP, as well as the development of their service sectors. I take this to corroborate the view that postindustrialization in all respects is best understood as a dimension added and related to the industrial dimension.

TABLE 4 **Government Proportion of GNP in Postindustrial and Industrial Societies (1965)**

Factor Grouping	No. Cases	Mean %	*F* Ratio (*F* Probability)
Postindustrial	14	14.85	4.63 (.017)
Industrial	27	12.03	. . .

postindustrial and industrial categories. Finally, table 4 tests the hypothesis that the countries listed in the postindustrial group of table 3 should devote higher proportions of their GNP to government than the countries in the industrial class. This is an important table, because I did not use the government sector in the factor analysis, and hence the table presents an opportunity for independent confirmation of the model. Using one-way analysis of variance, the table corroborates the view that postindustrial societies devote more attention to their government sectors.

The factor analysis and graphs provide provisional substantiation of the argument. However, there are a number of points that should provide guidance for the within- and cross-system ecological work that needs to be done.

Cross-national data comparability often presents the investigator with difficult problems. One partial solution is to compare rates of change or changing rates of change instead of absolute values. This has the merit of conforming more closely to the implications of the process assumption. For example, one would look for the change in the slope of the relationship between the service and the manufacturing sector's proportion of the GNP. The following comments note basic aspects of the measures and data sources for each concept.

Industry and the service sector. The intent is to tap measures which reflect the shift from an emphasis on the production and consumption of material (durable) goods to services. Countries differ in the way they measure components of the economy. For example, the Japanese census breaks economic activity down into basic primary (mining, forestry, agriculture), secondary (manufacturing, construction), and tertiary (transportation, service, and public) sectors, while Britain provides more detailed breakdowns that must be combined to match the Japanese classification. On the other hand, one may simply work with cross-time rate changes in measures that may differ but yet be assumed to top the same underlying dimension. (The same point applies to measures of labor force, urbanization, government budget data, riots, protests, etc.)

National infrastructure. Hypothesized here is a point in a society's development sequence when attention shifts from the construction of infrastructure items to their maintenance. The measurement problems of this concept are difficult because, for example, societies differ in their proportion of transportation accounted for by roads, rail, and aviation; moreover, a shifting emphasis in a nation's investment in these forms of transportation must be controlled for. This problem is an example of the measurement hazards attached to comparative and especially cross-time ecological analysis. Cross-time technological emphases change, and hence reliance on the railroad (per million-mile passenger or commercial tonnage) as an indicator of transportation would be an error in examining post-World War II transportation changes in the United States. The real problem is to know when to begin to shift emphasis in one's specific measures; I take this to be an important but essentially technical calibration problem.

5 From Scarcity to Abundance: The Impact of Cognitive Orientations on Politics

To understand better the politics of poverty in urban American settings, which primarily affects the black population, it is important to use the theoretical orientations of both American urbanists and cross-national specialists. In order to do this I shall develop a structuring principle (generated from a critique and extension of the concept of limited good) to account for behavior influenced by the culture of poverty. This concept was developed originally to explain peasant behavior in conditions of scarcity (Foster 1965). The structure of the argument here is based on the collective goods model presented in chapter 2.

My conclusion is that descriptions of the behavior, values, and attitudes of the American urban poor in terms of the culture of poverty concept really make sense only when we place them within relevant comparative findings providing a model to explain them. To reach this conclusion, I have taken the following steps: (1) analysis of the culture of poverty argument; (2) reformulation of the concept of limited good, using the assumption of individual rational choice and distinctions from the collective goods approach; and (3) location of the argument in a comparative framework with an assist from a model of collective action (Hirschman and Rothschild 1973, p. 566).

My collective goods model is based on the linkage between the degree of scarcity of goods and the cognitive orientations produced. I argue that whenever the environment is viewed as limited and nonincreasable in its yield, this produces a cognitive orientation known as the "image of limited good." Alternatively, if man views the environment producing his goods as expandable, an image of adequate good will be produced.

In its serious version, the culture of poverty explanation is cultural in form (Banfield 1958, 1970; Lewis 1970; Valentine 1968; and *Current Anthropology* 1969). The poor are unable to participate in the progress of the greater society because their socialization patterns (the culture of poverty) are incongruent with or nonproductive of a set of values and attitudes that promote a successful entry into the "developed" portion of society. While the argument does appear to describe much behavior in urban ghettos, the explanation itself is unsatisfactory because of the problems attached to cultural explanations in general. How does change ever occur if individuals are locked into a cultural belief system which structures their behavior?[1] Moreover, the culture of poverty thesis should stand the test of comparative examination of the political behavior of both rural peasants and the urban poor. However, although there are many examples which support the argument, there are also times when rural peasants do not act as the culture of poverty syndrome would predict, e.g., when they apparently do possess the cooperative and self-sacrificing values conducive to economic development, or when they revolt.

The confusion is due partly to the fact that two theoretical perspectives are used to examine specific cases and partly to standard comparative problems of concept formation, measurement, and selection and analysis of evidence. I shall try to explain the existence of the values and attitudes discussed by American urbanists and comparativists and show how they may be expected to differ at different social-economic development levels, with correspondingly different consequences for political behavior.

The Problem

I was led to develop the argument in this chapter after puzzling over important articles by Foster (1965, 1972) in which he develops the "image of limited good" in association with peasant societies. The concept he sought to develop assumed a closed system of economic scarcity. Under this condition Foster worked out a plausible explanation of peasant behavior by grouping their values and attitudes under the concept of cognitive orientation. The individual tends to make zero-sum calculations of gains and losses in his dealings with other members of the village, the unit which composes his universe. An economic gain for villager A is considered a loss for villager B. Foster argues that generally this perception has roots in reality. Under the conditions of thin survival margins that describe the subsistence agricultural conditions in which peasants live, individuals tend to compete for scarce resources. Foster's peasant is likely to exhibit values congruent with Banfield's characterization of the southern Italian peasant as amoral and his similar conception of urban blacks in the United States. Foster's peasant and Banfield's urban poor citizen are averse to long-range planning; i.e., they prefer the immediate gratification of wants to sacrificing for long-range goals; they are suspicious of outsiders, non-civic-minded, and both exploitative and exploited.

The interesting point is that while Foster's explicit central assumption is the notion of the individual as a rational, self-interested actor, neither he nor his commentators and critics (Foster 1972) appear to realize that the argument they are dealing with belongs essentially to the family of theories grouped under the collective goods heading.

The puzzle consists of two parts. First, it seemed to me that there are peasant societies that do not display dominant cognitive orientations consistent with Foster's "image of limited good." I include Tokugawa Japan; China before 1912; and perhaps portions of pre-industrial Europe. Many of these societies seemed to exhibit what I shall call the image of adequate good, even though the environment in which they existed appeared consistent with limited-good conditions. Second, what happens when the "image of limited good" wears off? As noted in chapter 1, we have two apparent sets of political responses in contemporary urban settings: the conditions which lead to perception of relative deprivation and increased political demand or the culture of poverty. I turn to the basic distinctions to be used in the argument.

Collective Goods, Cognitive Orientation, and Images of Goods

There are two additional points to emphasize in addition to the model of collective goods presented in chapter 2. First, it is important to note that, in treating preference schedules of individuals, the social environment must be characterized by the observer so that one may specify the context within which these individual schedules are developed (Riker and Ordeschook 1972, p. 6). Is the individual faced with a relatively simple set of choices afforded by a small group of political institutions, as in a peasant society, or a complex set of choices when confronted by political institutions in postindustrial states? The second point concerns our distinction between public and private goods at different levels of development. Some externalities may be ignored, while others drive individuals into collective action units. Pollution, for example, may be regarded as a necessary by-product of economic growth at one developmental level and an intolerable burden at another. Most important, however, in Foster's peasant society the production of goods is largely private, but this loses meaning in a society suffering resource scarcity, i.e., where the supply of all goods is sharply limited. This, then, is an instance of a good that is public in the sense of a shared production unit but supplied by individuals.

Foster's work suggests a way of reconciling cultural, social-psychological, and economic approaches with respect to the concept of value by modeling a cognitive orientation that, he argues, consists of the premises and assumptions by which individual behavior is structured: "All normative behavior is a function of their particular way of looking at their total environment, their unconscious acceptance of the 'rules of the game' in their cognitive orientation" (Foster 1965, p. 294). Rational behavior for the individual is simply operating competently within the cognitive orientation. Specific cognitive orientations are a function of the way individuals perceive their environment. Hence the "image of limited good" for peasants: "Broad areas of peasant behavior are patterned in such fashion as to suggest the peasants view their social, economic, and natural universes—their total environment—as one in which all of the desired things in life such as land, wealth, health, friendship and love, manliness and honor, respect and status, power and influence, security and safety, exist in finite quality and are always in short supply, as far as the peasant is concerned . . . there is no way *directly* within peasant power to increase the available quantity" (ibid., p. 296; emphasis added).

If goods are thought to exist in a limited and fixed quantity, improvement in A's state can come only at the expense of B. After giving examples to support his case, Foster moves from the individual to the collective level: "If . . . peasants see their universe as one in which the good things in life are limited and unexpandable quantities, and hence personal gain must be at the expense of others, we must assume that social institutions, personal behavior, values and personality, will all display patterns that can be viewed as functions of this cognitive orientation" (ibid., p. 301). For Foster's peasants, hard work and thrift are not accepted as basic elements of their cognitive orientations because additional hard work does not pay off.

If one accepts the rational-choice assumption as defined in chapter 2, what previously fell under the rubric of "cultural values" may be thought of as a stock of institutionalized survival strategies that in turn structure attitudes and behavior. This is because every society builds up its stock of norms and values through the interaction of groups and individuals with their environment. Once norms and values are institutionalized, they tend to endure in neutral or even mildly hostile environments. In general this is a function of the costs to the individual in making decisions. Unless there is a clear need, individuals will tend not to question existing values that structure their attitudes toward their world. Thus, in subsistence-level agricultural environments, it is reasonable to assume that peasants will tend to adopt a conservative posture toward change because of the absence of safety margins as a guard against the possible failure of innovations (Wise and Yotopoulos 1969). The risk of crop failure is not merely lower income or recourse to parity supports but starvation.

Foster's model is relevant to the impact of scarcity in several ways. He defines "scarcity" essentially as the absence of sufficient economic goods for adequate consumption standards. In a limited-good world, there are few incentives for any sort of collective action groups to form. It is rather like a Hobbesian world, because it is very difficult to develop a set of politically relevant game rules to maximize cooperative versus conflicting styles of resolution (Hardin 1968).

Although Foster argues that the "image of limited good" holds until societies reach a fairly high level of social-economic development, there are two problems with his argument that I must confront before reorganizing and extending the model to the culture of poverty literature. First, Foster argues that the image of limited good is so central a feature in the value system of peasants that the entire system must be transformed before a new image can be developed to supplant it. Yet is this accurate? Apparently in some peasant societies transformation of economic activity from a subsistence economy has occurred without total destruction of the dominant cognitive orientation (E. Williams 1970). In any event, some parts of the "image of limited good" are transformed to some other image at an unspecified point in the development process; how does this transformation occur, and what image emerges? Second, is Foster's model as generalized to all peasant societies as he would have it? Ethnographic studies of peasant societies in Japan, China, Korea, and Southeast Asia appear to describe groups in which scarcity of economic goods obtains (Nakane 1971). Yet they also suggest a different cognitive orientation, in which cooperative and consensual behavior dominate. Why is this the case? An answer may be provided if we return to the collective goods approach.

In chapter 2 I distinguished pure public from private goods. Foster is concerned primarily with small-scale (closed-system) societies in which political institutions are often latent rather than manifest: i.e., expressed within the code of village behavior and outlined in the society's cognitive orientation. Though the majority of goods in this kind of society would presumably be defined as private rather than public, the distinction breaks down in such situations, and all goods are treated as collective; and the main difficulty becomes the amount of goods supplied. There are not sufficient goods for the economy to operate efficiently enough for a market economy to succeed, and there are also no outside forces in central political institutions powerful enough to coerce peasants into changing their behavior. If enough goods were supplied, the market would theoretically operate more efficiently, and peasants would be encouraged to cooperate in economic and political endeavors. As the supply of goods expands, opportunities for consumption of private and public goods increases, and the impact of the limited-good image declines. Thus it is possible to construct at least one other image which may be posited as an alternative to the image of limited good: the image of adequate good.[2]

The adequate-good environment will produce an associated image that structures a similar cognitive orientation. The perception is the opposite of the image of limited good: that the environment will support an acceptable living standard if work tasks are divided and if individuals subordinate themselves to the group, work hard, and defer their desires for immediate gratification for long-range goals. While the environment may still appear harsh, the evidence suggests to the individual member of an adequate-good community that the condition of the collectivity and, more important, his own condition can continue to be improved because this has happened in the past.

As important as the positive incentives offered by perception of an adequate-good environment, which will reward work over time, is the range of weapons and potentially available to the leaders of hierarchical political structures that may exist above the individual (e.g., village leaders and regional and national leaders) to effect sanctions on the individual who deviates from accepted conduct. For example, within the village sanctions range from social pressures to conform to exile from the village—no small punishment in an uncertain and hostile world.

The introduction of the adequate-good image and political institutions into our closed peasant society creates the opportunity for individuals to break out of their previous image. This inference is supported by the theory of collective action (Olson 1965; and Frolich, Oppenheimer, and Young 1971), which suggests the conditions under which collective action will occur. Individuals who act rationally will not comply with the wishes of political elites to join collective action units unless there are strongly influential positive incentives or negative sanctions. Where resources are very scarce, there will be no incentives or sanctions available within the social system to ensure cooperative behavior; much of daily life is consumed by the need to gather food. But the incentives for cooperation increase as we move from a scarce to a limited and then to an adequate supply of goods. When individuals see the positive benefits of innovations in agriculture in terms of greater yields, they will adopt the innovations. However, Olson's emphasis on negative sanctions as well provides another clue as to when Foster's image of limited good is superseded; when the closed-system condition is relaxed and we begin to speak about penetrated systems, we see the conditions under which peasants are coerced into behavior congruent with the image of adequate good, even when Foster's limited-good image appears to be more appropriate. For instance, Nakane's (1971) description of Japanese peasant society deals with village social units in which a complex mix of incentives and sanctions ensures maximum individual work habits. These virtually self-contained social units (*buraku*) are in turn penetrated by the *daimyo* (lord) above. Village leaders owe allegiance, codified in their cognitive orientation, to their hierarchical superiors. Where one does not find this degree of organization, as in rural India, one finds behavior again congruent with Foster's limited-good image (Sen 1966).

Foster assumed a closed system when he developed his model, but when one relaxes the closed-boundary restriction and introduces the possibility of institutional intervention, a new set of parameters must be taken into account. Then we must look at the institutionalization level—the capacity of central political institutions to reach down to the village level in order to understand peasant societies in which Foster's image appears not to structure behavior. The presence or absence of strong central political institutions enables us to understand, with an assist from another collective goods model developed by Hirschman (Hirschman and Rothschild 1973), the reaction of urban poor to the condition of relative deprivation.

The Limited-Good Image in the Urban Setting

Foster's argument that the limited-good image is the dominant cognitive orientation of peasants throughout a substantial portion of the development process must be altered if one accepts the existence of the adequate-good image. As soon as economic development begins and peasants move into urban areas, the conditions for relative deprivation are met. While peasants' lives may be yet governed by the limited-good image, evidence around them suggests an alternative, the image of adequate good. This, then, would appear to be the point at which a sharp rise in political demands should occur; in fact it is the point at which things become confused. In some societies the urban poor appear to fall under the limited-good image, while other examples provide evidence, through demonstrations, riots, and strikes, that the effects of the relative-deprivation hypothesis (Gurr 1970) have set in.[3] However, we are now also in a position to offer an alternative explanation for the culture of poverty thesis. For the majority of American blacks, by far the largest portion of our urban poor, the opportunities necessary for the image of adequate good to prevail are absent. One need only refer to their chronic level of unemployment, their associated housing and health difficulties, etc., to view in a different light their corresponding apparent emphasis on immediate gratification of desires: emphasis on violence, alcoholism, and other "pathologies" (so defined by the dominant middle class). I would place the cognitive orientation that structures such behavior under a contemporary urban version of the image of limited good. The question is why there is no violent protest or revolution under these conditions, since urban American blacks, and their equivalents in other countries, do not live in isolation—the enemy is proximate and conditions are ripe for perception of relative deprivation.

The fact is, Hirschman argues, that groups often do tolerate substantial and even rising economic and social inequalities when development begins. To account for this, Hirschman sketches his "tunnel effect." Imagine yourself in a tunnel in an automobile in the left of two lanes of waiting cars; if the cars in the right lane begin to move while your lane remains blocked, what is your reaction—anger? No, answers Hirschman; relief and happy expectation. You may feel a twinge of irritation at the fact that the right lane is moving ahead first, but this emotion is outweighed by the positive feeling that you may expect to move ahead too in the near future. This set of cognitive orientations toward economic growth prevails when economic development begins. The question then becomes one of the conditions under which the tunnel effect will last or decay. This is important because when decay sets in, i.e., when one realizes that one's line is not going to move, the effects described by the relative-deprivation hypothesis set in and, other things being equal, political demands rise. Hirschman lays out the following conditions for the continuation of the tunnel effect. First, the group that does not advance "must be able to empathize, at least for a while, with the group that does advance" (Hirschman and Rothschild 1973, p. 554). If the economic advance is associated with a different group, in terms of ethnicity, religion, or language, the stalled group may make the opposite prediction to that implied in the tunnel effect—they will expect to become worse off. Clearly in most contemporary societies, even if individuals live in a limited-good environment, advances in communication afford them the opportunity to learn about the possibility of an adequate-good world.[4]

But what about American ghetto blacks who, if I am correct, inhabit a limited-good world in the midst of a surrounding adequate-good environment? Certainly the American black is warranted in assuming that time has run out in the tunnel. Why does he not revolt instead of retaining or resigning himself to the limited-good image? Of course, one answer lies in examining what is meant by domestic violence and how it is distinguished from revolution. Returning to our model, we may place intragroup violence of all types in the limited-good matrix and externally directed violence in the junction between limited- and adequate-good images, at the point when, as Hirschman describes it, the tunnel effect wears off. If one analyzes the domestic violence in the United States from this approach, black activity has been mainly encompassed in the limited-good image. Urban riots have resulted in the destruction of black, not white, neighborhoods; black, not white, lives (Cloward and Piven 1974). The potential leaders of the black community experiencing stirrings of a change from limited to adequate orientations are coopted by the group that already operates under the adequate-good image, the white middle class. Thus what positive incentives are there for the former group to revolt? And there are unambiguous negative sanctions present in the form of a massive law enforcement system poised to punish transgressors, i.e., anyone who would commit intergroup violence. In contrast, by and large the state is prepared to ignore the "pathologies" of the ghetto. Urban blacks are essentially confined, by spatial boundaries in the form of inaccessible suburbs and economic isolation, in a limited-good world as securely as their peasant Third World counterparts.[5]

Perhaps it is useful to illustrate the argument. Figure 8 juxtaposes revolutionary and culture of poverty (limited-good) violence: the higher the one, the lower the other. If the argument presented here is accurate, Hirschman's suggestion about the way attitudes toward inequalities change is more useful than that of the relative-deprivation J-curve adherents. The problem changes from one of the scar-

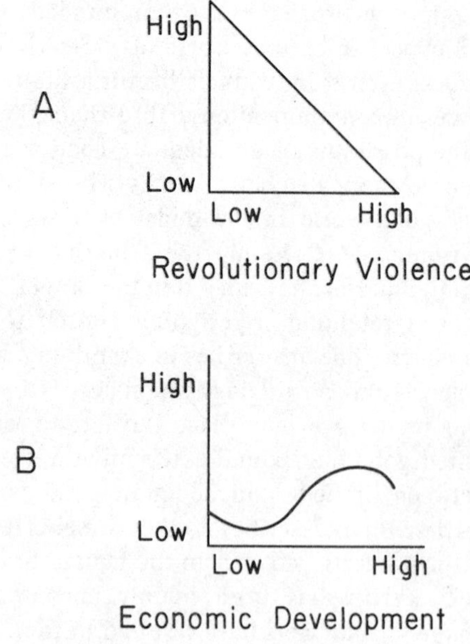

Fig. 8. Culture of poverty violence (*A*) versus revolutionary violence (*B*).

city itself to the perception of inequality in the distribution of resources. If we add the collective action–based argument about the difficulties of urban blacks when faced with strong political institutions that can deal effectively with attacks in addition to presenting a favored few with incentives to migrate from their community, we can transform the J-curve to an S-curve; revolutionary violence does not rise until well into the development period (because of Hirschman's tunnel effect), at which point it inclines sharply but then declines if the political institutions surmount the challenge. For urban blacks there is a return to the contemporary version of the image of limited good at this juncture.[6]

The pattern is as follows. The image of limited good carries over until the peasants perceive the possibility of an adequate-good environment. This point is not reached until there has been substantial movement from rural to urban areas and enough economic development for a representative developing group to become easily identifiable. At this point, as in a branching exercise, either Hirschman's tunnel effect takes hold, and a more or less long period of tolerance for economic growth with inequality ensues, or there will be an immediate move toward increasing political demands on the existing regime, demands scaled up to and including revolutionary violence. Eventually Hirschman's tunnel effect wears off, and a sharp rise in political demands occurs. The political institutions may or may not meet the challenge, depending on their level of institutionalization. If the disadvantaged group does not succeed, another version of the limited-good image will become dominant.

Conclusion

There are both theoretical and policy implications worthy of study which can be only noted here. The most general theoretical claim put forth is that when we model environmental perceptions of individuals in terms of the mix of incentives for and sanctions against collective action, we may account for both "public-regarding" and individualistic behavior with the same set of rationality assumptions. This means that the burden of noncooperative behavior and the absence of the deferred-gratification pattern is removed from the individual, where it resides in the culture of poverty thesis, and placed on external structural (environmental and institutional) conditions. Norms and values, the stuff of cultural explanations, should be treated as descriptive evidence, i.e., as guides to the existing specific mix of collective action sanctions and incentives rather than as adequate explanations of social-economic and political phenomena.

There are public policy questions that should be addressed as well. Is it in fact possible, in highly interdependent postindustrial societies, for parts rather than all of the dominant cognitive orientation of a group to be transformed in order for that group to avoid "cultural genocide?" Are there incentive versus sanction options left for political leaders that are congruent with American liberal democratic values and still potentially useful in dealing with urban poverty? To pose only two basic questions as examples is not to present their solutions, but perhaps the discussion has been useful in redirecting our attention to the assumptions and theoretical models which we use in thinking about the culture of poverty thesis that underlies them.

* * *

"A transformation may be taking place in the political cultures of advanced industrial societies. This transformation seems to be altering the basic value priorities of given generations, as a result of changing conditions influencing their basic socialization. The changes seem to affect the stand one takes on current political issues and may have a long-term tendency to alter existing patterns of political partisanship" (Inglehart 1971, p. 991).

The question posed by Inglehart is whether we may account for the value change apparently emerging in postindustrial societies with the model presented in the following chapter. I shall try to show that, just as we may postulate a plausible model to account for the set of values that appear consistent with the industrial phase of sociopolitical change—i.e., a propensity for deferred gratification, subordination of the individual to the group and to larger social, economic, and political institutions in society—we may use the same analytics to interpret the value change in postindustrial society toward the primacy of the individual over the group and larger institutions, concern for individual sociopsychological desires, and often the immediate gratification of those desires.

In fact individual transformation from the limited- to the adequate-good image corresponds to system transformation to the mature industrialization phase of sociopolitical change. Here, represented by the peak of industrial dominance of the economy, the environment is most expressive of the image of adequate good.

Individuals working in concert (epitomized in the assembly line) produce and consume material goods in their greatest amount compared with other goods.

The adequate-good image becomes progressively less dominant as a society moves into the postindustrial process-state, for several reasons. (1) While the environment may continue to be viewed as expandable, at least in part, economic growth during the industrial phase may not have reduced economic inequalities (*Royal Commission on the Distribution of Income and Wealth* 1975). (2) Because postindustrialization apparently involves an absolute decline in the rate of economic growth, this may move perception of the environment for some in the direction of the zero-sum world of the previous limited-good image. (3) In addition, the change is consistent with the rational-choice assumption about individual preferences that would suggest that when basic adequate goods are supplied, individual attention turns to qualitative wants—a hallmark of postindustrial societies. Moore puts it thus:

> It is often claimed that scarcity can never be eliminated because human wants are inherently unlimited. This argument is not convincing. If human wants were essentially unlimited, it is highly unlikely that modern society would have developed the whole apparatus of advertising to create more and more wants. Furthermore, at the level of straightforward biological needs, such as those of sleep, food, and sex, there is an obvious upper limit of satiation. More subtle cultural and psychological needs, such as those for affection and admiration, do not have such clear upper limits. On the other hand, these vary with changing historical conditions. How they will be affected by the future of industrial society is an open question to which both pessimistic and optimistic answers are possible. [B. Moore 1965, pp. 184–85]

The image emerging beyond that of the adequate good is likely to be much more complex, both in reality and as a model. At the most basic level, the cognitive orientation produced beyond the adequate good will emphasize the values suggested by writers on the subject. Since the individual may assume the acceptable standard of living produced by his subordination to the group and by deferral of immediate gratification in favor of the pursuit of long-range goals, he will no longer be content with an adequate level of existence but will demand a better quality of work experience and gratification of personal wants formerly suppressed, and he will emphasize his claims over those of the group and larger institutions. Here I will make some projection about the changes in cognitive orientations beyond the adequate good.

First, because of increasing interdependence, the slowing of economic growth, and accelerating costs of government, citizens increasingly view actions of other individuals, groups, and institutions as implying potential costs rather than benefits to themselves. Fewer dimensions of the environment are seen as neutral, as social and economic systems of increasing complexity leave unaffected fewer areas of activity concerning humans. If postindustrialization is the period when collective goods dominate, it is also the period when negative spillover effects drive individuals into collective action units. Second, the images of limited and adequate good assume development, a term avoided in this book, to be dominated by material wealth concerns. However, development may be redefined to incorporate the concept of postindustrialization and hence new problems and possibilities for the individual to confront.

6 Choice, Development, and the Political Consequences of Postindustrialization

Even if one does not make unilinear assumptions about societies necessarily moving through stages of development, if specific societies have moved beyond "development" into postindustrialization, it is important to reconceptualize the concept of "development." This is so because understandings attached to such concepts remain compelling images upon which subsequent research about all points in the political change process is built. I examine the implications of viewing development in terms of individual choice directed at primary wants that change in concert with environmental change from modernization to postindustrialization. Changes in wants across the development process compel changes in instruments to make wants accessible: I argue that it is useful to view material goods, time, space, energy, and information as shifting ratios of wants and instrumentalities. Postindustrialization is the phase in which information, itself a chief instrument in the industrialization process-state, becomes a primary want; the *search* for solution becomes the major problem for individual choice, along with the need for a solution itself.

Development has been usefully characterized as the expansion of individual choice (Apter 1965, 1971; Inkeles and Smith 1974). However, the nature of this choice remains unspecified across systems (cross-national) and across time.[1] If it is reasonable to assume that choice is governed by individual wants (needs), it becomes important to examine the prime determinants of wants. I shall argue here that those wants are a function of the individual's relationship with the environment, which I will define in terms of the concept of cognitive orientation. The argument links the methodological individualism assumption of rational choice to a description of primary wants shifting across the process of sociopolitical change. The specific nature of the cognitive orientation is a function of (*a*) the level and type of environmental scarcity conditions and (*b*) the nature and condition of basic instruments available to make individual wants accessible. At the macro level, if it is clear that several societies have moved beyond the industrialization process-state (Bell 1973; Huntington 1974; Inglehart 1971; and Touraine 1974), the meaning(s) we attach to the concept of development should be reformulated for these societies. Moreover, even though I do not assume that any particular society will move through a predetermined set of changes, the realization that specific societies in the process of sociopolitical change have moved beyond industrialization has implications for our conceptualization of the other process-states previously identified as modernization and industrialization.

I conclude that development may be conceived of, from the perspective of individual choice, as changing primary use of material goods, energy, time, space, and information as basic access instruments to wants (goals). Similarly, the primary wants one wishes to satisfy also change. Thus I view individual choice as bounded by parameters that, in interaction with the environment, provide upper limits to the use of any single instrument and any particular primary set of wants. The implication is that "development," with its attendant social-economic and political consequences, may be conceived of as a series of shifting unidimensional curves, curvelinear or S-shaped, that chart the use of instruments shifting wants across time and the sociopolitical change process. In postindustrial societies information itself becomes the chief want individuals must deal with; the *search* for the solution becomes more costly than the solution itself. In order to reach this conclusion, the following steps are taken. (1) I characterize the individual, the environment (a description of the macro social-economic and political process, including the postindustrial process-state), and their relationships; (2) next, a model is developed in which the concepts of instrument, access, and primary wants are defined; and (3) the instruments are presented; (4) finally, the political implications of the argument are discussed.

The Basic Concepts and the Model

I have argued that postindustrialization allows us to complete, provisionally, the growth metaphor stated most succinctly by Huntington (1971); postindustrialization is the period in which the implications of that growth are dealt with (cf. chap. 4; see also Benjamin 1977).

The environment is composed of all elements—physical, social, and cultural—within which the individual operates. The physical environment, with the attendant goods it yields, places boundaries on individual choice in the sense that conditions of extreme scarcity will override individual nonmaterial wants. I have treated earlier the concept of cognitive orientation. It is important to recall that the argument suggests that specific cognitive orientations are constructed in response to the way individuals view their environment and that the concept of environment, for the individual, includes the actual premises upon which he perceives his environment. Because of information costs attached to the reconception of values and norms, individuals will choose not to question their cognitive orientation unless the environment becomes destructive of it. The task, then, is to model changes in the environment across modernization, industrialization, and postindustrialization to suggest the mix of incentives and sanctions requiring changes in individual cognitive orientations.

Of the myriad concepts of development, viewing it, like Apter, as the expansion of individual choice is closest to the position taken here.[2] Apter sees modernization as a process in which the choices presented to individuals are expanded. From the tightly bounded subsistence-equilibrium world of the peasant to the change-oriented world of the modern urban dweller, there is an enormous expansion of choices in all areas. The difficulty with Apter's concept concerns the question of upper limits. Surely it must be the case that time and space are not limitless parameters within which individual choice operates. In fact there are upper limits on (*a*) the number of personal relationships an individual can have; (*b*) the number, though not the quality, of experiences he can enjoy; (*c*) the goods he can consume; and (*d*) the information he can process and hold.[3] Whereas Apter is concerned primarily with the developmental process-state, in which the cognitive orientation of man changes over to change and growth, I shall focus on the postindustrial process-state, in which upper limits on some choices alternatives are being reached because of interdependence and resulting externalities.

The primary goals (wants) individuals set for themselves shift across time mainly as a function of basic environmental changes. All wants may be broken down into material and nonmaterial, e.g., social-psychological, categories. The hierarchies of needs and drives noted by psychologists are descriptions of the changing foci of individuals; once basic shelter, clothing, and food wants are relatively satisfied, attention turns sequentially to material comforts, social-psychological concerns, and finally moral needs. However, my task here is to specify plausible linkages between opportunities for new basic wants afforded by the environment and the primary instruments on which individuals focus to achieve them.

First I must specify the concept of instrument. Instruments are the basic means by which man achieves his wants, and thus they compose the arena of interest in a discussion of development as individual choice across time.[4] Changes in instruments (themselves evolving with environmental change) present new basic problems and opportunities for individual choice. This is so because concentration upon or exploitation of one instrument at one point in the process eventually leads to its overuse, whereupon it may become a net liability rather than an asset; its costs then lead to a search for new instruments to solve primary access problems. Overuse of instruments may also result in their transformation into primary wants. I shall now attempt to develop this general point by characterizing the primary instruments used across time. To reiterate, the distinction between instruments and primary wants is analytic rather than concrete. As soon as enough of a primary need is supplied to move the good from limited to adequate status, other subordinate wants become primary. At this point individuals must begin to work with new instruments to solve different access problems. *When scarce, material goods, time, space, energy, and information are basic wants; when sufficient or abundant, they become access instruments to new wants.*

Material goods. Assurance of an adequate supply of material goods from the environment is man's first imperative, and when minimum levels are secure, these become the base from which he procures other wants. The material goods question before us is adequacy of supply, not whether goods are jointly or privately produced and consumed. The literature on modernization describes the initial destabilizing impact of industrialization as heightening individual concern for food, clothing, and shelter. However, as a society reaches mature industrialization, individual emphasis on the production of material goods begins to shift to services. At this point the individual's chief instrument becomes energy and subsequently information. In fact, at the macroeconomic level, there is a point at which a relative decline begins in the dominance of the material-good sector over the economy; once the national infrastructure is established, once a society's housing needs are fulfilled, once the "potential" market for durable goods has been reached, individual attention turns to the attainment of other goals. Moreover, precisely when the positive utility of additional material goods begins to decline, their negative production costs begin to outweigh their benefits. I will return to this point below in treating information.

Time. Observers note the circularity of life's rhythm for peasants who perform seasonal agricultural activities (Inkeles and Smith 1974). The consensus of this literature is that the effect of the change metaphor (Huntington 1971) is to change the individual's concept from a nonlinear view of time, from a virtually unbroken and naturally ordered rhythm, to an ever increasingly "chunked" periodization. Certainly one of man's problems is the continuous necessity to adjust internal clocks to the imperatives of perpetual rationalization, bureaucratization, transportation and communication requirements, and indeed the whole of urban life itself. Underlying this view of changes in the individual's concept of time throughout modernization is of course the related assumption that the imperatives of industrialization require that change. In fact it is difficult to visualize industrial plants operating without careful consideration of time and motion dimensions which often require split-second accuracy. And the bureaucratization of life implies meetings, which increases organization of one's time in a chronological as well as efficiency sense. Entry into industrial, technological, or other components of the service system requires extensive preparation; in many professional activities individuals do not become effectively productive until they approach thirty years of age. This underlies the societal organization of citizens' preproduction years into a set of educational intervals, beginning with elementary school and ending with postgraduate work. Moreover, other hierarchical social and economic institutions then divide the individual lifetime into similar "linear" chunks, producing Whyte's (1957) lament of the organization man. However, the conclusion seems inescapable that time is a primary access instrument to individual wants, mainly material in nature, during the modernizing and industrializing phases of sociopolitical change and that this instrument is used for purposes of choice through its gradual, increasing organization.

The question is whether there are upper limits to the rationalization of time from the individual's perspective. Just as there are apparently limitations to sequences of numbers that man can retain in memory (G. Miller 1956), is it not possible that there are similar limitations to individual tolerance of organization of his time? Surely there is a point at which continued efforts to increase use of time for access purposes becomes counterproductive, at which costs begin to outweigh benefits in an economic if not a psychological sense. Coincidental with the onset of postindustrialization, the effort to guard against the negative consequences of routinization of the individual's time begins. This is because there is a point beyond which the use of time—its continued rationalization—as a primary resource is no longer of positive aid to the individual in procuring wants but becomes a negative externality (spillover effect), a problem in and of itself. In this sense, then, it is reasonable to argue that the upper limits of the use of time are reached.

Energy. Perhaps as important as his need to procure goods is man's need to develop inanimate energy sources to produce these goods. One definition of development describes the onset of modernization as the change in the ratio of inanimate to animate energy sources (Levy 1966). Whenever this occurs, an apparently exponential increase in the production and consumption of energy begins. And yet here also one may project (in reality it has happened nowhere yet, to my knowledge) first a slowdown of the rate of increase in energy production and consumption, then a gradual leveling off of its increase, followed by the attainment of an equilibrium of energy production and consumption. There are several reasons for this. Once a relatively high level of production of material goods is reached, economic attention turns to the service (especially the public) sector, where information, not energy, is both the primary access instrument to individual wants and a basic want itself. This point may be accented if the identifying characteristic of postindustrialization as the age of information is correct. However, in addition to the positive incentives that shift individual attention from an emphasis on material to service-related wants, familiar environmental constraints apparently provide upper limits to the continued expansion of energy production.

Space. During the modernization process, virtually equal in importance to the shift from a circular to a linear view of time is the use of spatial solutions to procure wants that are material in nature. The spatial solution, urbanization, is closely linked to the process of industrialization itself. If the latter involves the development of standardized solutions to a variety of manufacturing problems, symbolized by the assembly line, there must exist easily obtainable solutions to the nonstandard problems of equipment breakdown, interruption of supply of raw materials, and other special difficulties, in order to avoid loss of plant time. Generally this has meant the use of space as a chief instrument for access purposes. Urbanization is thus interpretable as a solution to important economic problems. In order to defeat the logistical problem of transportation and communication, man creates the modern city; workers live near plants, service companies are proximate, and alternative sources of raw materials can be found. We are familiar with the urban sprawl of London, Paris, New York, and Tokyo; and even larger cities are on the way. However, urban (spatial) solutions to production problems peak and then decline; this is already the case in the postindustrial societies. Witness the megalopolitan array from Boston to Washington in the United States and, we might add, London to Hamburg in Europe. High-technology companies increasingly locate in rural areas. The reasons for this change are (*a*) the solution to the transportation problems attached to locating away from an urban center and (*b*) the development of technologies to assist the exchange of needed information. In the language of economics, economies of scale no longer necessarily accrue to those adopting spatial solutions for their economic difficulties. This includes white-collar bureaucratic areas of economic activity as well as manufacturing. Computers, information retrieval systems, information terminals all allow service and especially public bureaucracies to be located without reference to proximity, the condition solved by the urban setting. Hence it is possible to understand the emerging importance of information as the chief instrument of access to wants.

Information. In the postindustrial phase of sociopolitical change, information becomes the primary individual access instrument for a number of reasons. If the basic focus of the economy changes from the manufacturing to service, information becomes the primary ingredient in individual choice. In fact another way to define the service sector of the economy is in terms of information:

services permit individuals access to wants; services thus may be conceived of as an instrument.[5] One theorist sees knowledge itself (defined in research and development terms) as the major structuring principle denoting the onset of postindustrialization (Bell 1973). Social-psychological wants require different solutions, which suggests the importance of information itself to discover possible solutions, if the access route is known *and* one has the means to use it. If increasingly differentiated wants emerge, individuals begin to find information costs supplanting energy or spatial costs; the search for the answer itself becomes the issue. At this point the increasing cost of information begins to make it a primary want; the relevance of the market mechanism, as classically defined, declines. Let us note the reasons for this transformation. First, however, note the positive incentives that have moved individuals toward information as the chief instrument. Here technology itself effects threshold changes in the way men interact. The virtually exponential increase in the complexity, scope, reliability, and ease of access of information systems themselves is the most compelling technological feature of postindustrialization. Information systems allow individuals to conceive of satisfying spatial wants (e.g., tourism) at low individual costs and a high degree of reliability. The communication, storage, and retrieval of information via traditional libraries is rapidly becoming obsolete, and we are now beginning the task of adapting our academic, social, and economic institutions to the possibilities afforded by information technology.

The major property that changes information into a primary want derives from the presence of postindustrialization itself. One of its defining characteristics is interdependence, which increases possible negative as well as positive connections between individuals and groups. Conditions giving rise to negative connections (1) compel citizens to expend much time and energy procuring information necessary to deal with appropriate units within large and continuously expanding public and private institutions and (2) lead individuals to attempt to control access by others to information in their possession.

The numerous conditions in each category will only be summarized here. In the city the costs of living in close proximity begin to outweigh benefits when (*a*) an individual's economic benefits begin to wane and (*b*) he feels an excessive impingement by others in terms of noise and air pollution, traffic and housing congestion, etc. If given the opportunity, he exits to the suburbs at this point. Postindustrialization is defined by the rise of the public sector and a concomitant rise of other social and economic institutions that both control and serve an increasing number of human needs. Especially in the case of the public sector, we are talking about the absence of market mechanisms that supply the potential buyer and seller with necessary information in an efficient manner; citizens are compelled to extend substantial amounts of their own time and energy as information costs. The information needs of collective action units mount and eventually become a net cost to citizens, a burdensome negative externality. Moreover, the information system itself presents increased opportunities for individuals or groups to manipulate other individuals or groups for whatever purpose they might have. This is why security of privileged information becomes a central political issue in the computerized postindustrial age. In fact many individuals and groups will be unable to "afford" the necessary information to fulfill their wants. In any event, it is possible to conceive of the rise of information as a primary want itself.

A related supporting argument is provided by the distinction developed between material and positional goods (Hirsch 1976). If we assume material goods to be basically private in nature, positional goods are primarily collective, limited, and not produceable at will. Whereas individual X's consumption of material goods usually does not impinge on the consumption of like goods by individual Y, the consumption of positional goods tends to be more like a zero-sum game, i.e., like a nonexpanding economy. One's enjoyment of a national park is in part dependent on the exclusion of others from the setting. Enjoyment of one's villa on the French Riviera depends on limiting the right of others to own similar villas in close proximity. As material wealth expands, the attractiveness of many positional goods declines. "As a middle class professional remarked when cheap charter flights opened up a distant exotic country: 'Now that I can afford to come here I know that it will be ruined'" (ibid., p. 167). To the extent that postindustrialization may be identified with the rise of positional relative to material goods, this creates an additional set of collective action incentives for individuals. Under such conditions of *relative* material abundance on one hand and the nature of positional goods on the other, information as the chief instrument of access to wants becomes crucial. Thus in an increasingly complex world the cost of the search for the access instrument appropriate to one's wants is the main issue. This is true especially for positional goods which are highly information sensitive, in that a large amount of contextual information is required before one can determine the particular positional goods that meet one's preferences. Moreover, information about them is biased toward those who already possess positional advantage.

Implications and Conclusion

There are a number of permutations of the instruments and basic wants surveyed in this discussion. In one sense, man attends to all of these elements, if only to maintain them in equilibrium. However, it is the changing emphasis from one process-state to another that distinguishes basic choice problems (wants) for individuals. There are a number of additional implications.

1. If information is the primary access instrument to positional and collective goods, are present political institutions capable of responding to increased demands on them? The basically centralized social and political institutions constructed during and for the industrialization phase of sociopolitical change may not prove adaptable to the postindustrial phase, in which the types of goods delivered by government change from basic "pure" public goods to collective goods. I have noted earlier that goods that are more information sensitive (requiring more sender-receiver interactions) require government institutions of different sizes for delivery purposes. The postindustrial world, for example, is populated by highly informed, discrete groups (catchments) that demand more than a *general* health care policy; they each demand a policy tailored to their particular needs.

2. However, if goods themselves are different, what are the optimum sizes of (*a*) their government delivery units and (*b*) their catchment(s)? These problems cannot be solved easily, but if they are the appropriate questions, redesign of government institutions must be placed first on the agenda in postindustrial societies. If space and time are no longer primary access instruments, it is likely that the government units designed to relate to them are not particularly relevant to the political problems caused by the rise of information as the chief instrument and subsequent want.

3. Information and the ability to acquire it become the primary means by which individuals may be distinguished; in fact we are in a position to add to the definition of social class and status itself. The

greater the ability of the individual to provide for different wants through multiple information systems, the higher his social level. Recall Boulding's (1956) metaphor of the image: one's ability to gain access to wants is dependent on the possible images one is able to code and retain internally. Two individuals may live side by side with equal incomes and yet lead very different lives. X may be content to develop relationships and economic ties locally and thus procure fewer social and cultural wants. In comparison, Y may travel, gain access to many varied social and cultural wants, and develop primarily national and international professional and social relationships.[6]

4. If the analytic distinctions about individual choice and development have merit, no single notion of choice entirely captures the development process. Rather, it emphasizes that there are upper limits to particular wants and instruments. As soon as individuals reach unidentified points of consumption or specific use of time, space, etc., there is a change in order of preference in favor of another want. The discussion proceeding from the individual reminds us that he is a bounded unit with limited time, ability to absorb and control information, and use for goods and energy and spatial instruments.[7]

In sum, my major claim is that development, from the perspective of individual choice, really comprises changing mixes of primary wants and instruments to those wants. However, there are upper limits—saturation points—to the use of any particular instrument, beyond or before which it may be a primary want to be dealt with in itself. For example, societies that may be characterized as postindustrial today used available energy sources in the past for purposes of industrialization without much thought to their replenishment. Now energy is becoming more of a want than an instrument. In earlier stages the cost of information was low relative to the cost of basic material goods, spatial solutions, etc. However, in the postindustrial phase, although technology provides unparalleled opportunities for the communication of information, the design of present basic social-economic and political institutions inhibits effective use of this technology. In an interdependent world in which externalities (positive and negative) increasingly impinge on the individual, information about his preferences becomes more important. Negative spillover effects on individuals from pollution, inequalities of income distribution, public goods differentially distributed—all drive individuals into collective action units which then increase the load or overload on governmental institutions (King 1975). The resulting increased political activity creates increased information uncertainty across levels of government and between government and citizen. The increase in the importance of positional goods also results in increased political conflict and corresponding information problems.

Finally, the concept of development posited here suggests a process-based view that the absence of problems is simply not a part of development viewed from the perspective of individual choice. We must be alert to environmental changes promoting changes in individual preference orderings in the manner outlined here. This also means that once information costs are reduced, we should expect other primary problems to surface. At present we should be concerned with the apparent inability of political institutions developed for the industrial phase to reduce information costs.

7 Pluralism and Corporatism: Misplaced Models for Postindustrial Politics

It is curious only to the intelligent layman that specialists in American politics and comparative politics continue to develop and refine concepts, models, approaches, and theories of politics in virtual isolation from each other. In a superficial sense, the difference between the two sets of specialists may be due simply to a variant of the forest and trees metaphor. Indeed the student of American politics is awash in individual- and group-level data, inundated by an enormous outpouring of research on all possible politically relevant topics, and he is perhaps excessively attached to questions of technique and method. Few work on the macro level of analysis, the American political system. In contrast, the comparative politics specialist is still likely to be a generalist with respect to the politics of his country of study. Because of a traditional emphasis on the nation-state level of analysis, the student of comparative politics remains more likely to ask broad questions concerning the total polity. Moreover, it would not be erroneous to say that there is much less research of all types available on all countries outside the United States than within the American setting on America. However, there have been recent attempts by comparative specialists to elaborate the concept of corporatism as a structuring principle to understand the basic workings of politics, primarily in western European and other authoritarian societies. These attempts allow us to juxtapose corporatism and pluralism, which remains the dominant assumption or metaphor structuring understanding of American politics. Like pluralism, corporatism is built on assumptions, understandings, and predictions about interest groups as central features in the political process. The point of initial connection with this work is of course collective goods theory and, more specifically, the collective action theory of interest groups first outlined by Olson (1965).

My conclusion is that pluralism and corporatism are design principles generated for and differentially applicable to societies up to and including mature industrialization, but not beyond. In fact the achievement itself of the smooth political consensus envisaged by the corporatist thinkers sets the stage for its decline. Far from being an enduring form of political organization, corporatism really represents a political transition point between industrialization and postindustrialization.

Pluralism

If there is a name to be attached to the principles underlying the thought and actions of political theorists and practitioners in the United States, it remains pluralism. From the *Federalist Papers* (especially Madison's no. 10) to recent efforts (Dahl 1961; and Polsby 1963), the prevailing emphasis concerning the workings of American politics has been on interest groups; politics consists of conflict between interest groups over scarce resources in a public arena. The conflict is overseen by a legislative body which ratifies the monetary victories of one coalition over others, a judiciary that acts as rule keeper, and an executive branch that enforces these rules and provides administrative remedies for policies ordered changed by Congress. Pluralism is based on a pessimistic view of man's ability to plan the affairs of others, rise above the dictates of self-interests, etc. A democratic key to the pluralist concept is the notion of open access of individuals—through groups—to the political arena. Because of this and an underlying consensus about the viability, the superiority, of this system of government, strong majority support of it was thought to develop. Thus the view is often expressed that American politics is based on a positive attitude toward consensus and that an underlying equilibrium characterizes the American political system.[1] One of the most discerning students and critics of the concept summarizes the optimistic faith still apparent in most pronouncements about pluralism: "(1) Groups, of which corporations are merely one type, possess power directly over a segment of society and also a share of control of the state. (2) Groups, rather than entrepreneurs and firms, are the dominant reality in modern life. (3) As long as even a small proportion of all interests remains strong and active, no unitary class, or 'power elite,' will emerge. That is, in the pluralist system it is highly improbable that a consensus across a whole class can last long enough to institutionalize itself" (Lowi 1969, p. 45). Contemporary society is thought much too complex for a single power elite to form, and there are many decision-making centers scattered throughout society. Finally, an additional emphasis on liberty, self-government, and hence aversion to planning is noted by another recent commentator on pluralism:

> Massive endorsement of the private association as an essential of democracy is one of the most striking features of American political thought. Freedom of association has virtually become a fundamental guarantee of the Constitution. The ideas of self-government and self-regulation have entered deeply into the doctrines of the political order, and they have been industrialized to an unheralded degree. The private association, moreover, has been linked with the values of decentralization and federalism. It has also been pictured as the source of stability in politics and held up as the medium of public interest. Most frequently, however, it has been seen as the guarantor of liberty. [McConnell 1966, p. 119]

Now both of our writers, Lowi and McConnell, present cogent criticism of the descriptive and explanatory validity of pluralism with respect to contemporary American society and politics. Even if the reality of American politics was once captured by pluralism, post–World War II America belies that description. In fact monopolistic oligarchies in business, government itself in its various large bureaucracies, and unions all really combine to "solve" political problems. The shifting set of interest-group coalitions envisaged by pluralists does not occur; in fact the open access required by pluralists is gone, and something different has taken its place. Again, Lowi states the properties of what he calls interest-group liberalism:

> It may be called liberalism because it expects to use government in a positive and expansive role, it is motivated by the highest sentiments, and it possesses strong faith that what is good for government is good for the society. It is "interest group liberalism" because it sees as both necessary and good that the policy agenda and the public interest be defined in terms of the organized interests of society. . . . It assumes: (1) Organized interests are homogeneous and easy to define, sometimes monolithic. . . . (2) Organized interests pretty much fill up and adequately represent most of the sectors of our lives, so that one organized group can be found effectively answering and checking some other organized group as it seeks to prosecute its claims against society.

> And (3) the role of government is one of ensuring access particularly to the most effectively organized, and of ratifying the agreements and adjustments worked out among the competing leaders and their claims. . . . Taken together these assumptions constitute the Adam Smith "hidden hand" model applied to groups. [P. 71]

McConnell paints a similar picture of the realities of the American political system and views the accent on organized interests critically because of the decline of democracy which results. Far from ensuring democracy, pluralism freezes the privileges of existing interests that support a highly stratified society—one in which the poor, the unorganized, lose out. Moreover, this excessive concentration on the support of fragmentary private interests inhibits development of policy supporting the public interest. For McConnell, decentralization itself is unfortunate because it "will generally tend to accentuate any inequality in the distribution of power that would otherwise exist within each decentralized unit" (p. 107). In support of this point, McConnell notes Michel's "iron law of oligarchy" and the work of Olson (1965) that he feels suggests that smaller groups are more likely to be undemocratic and that weaker interest groups are not competitive with stronger interest groups. For his part, Lowi presents a sweeping indictment of the political implications of interest-group liberalism. He argues that it has failed to produce effective domestic or foreign planning in virtually every important public policy area. Moreover, social-economic inequities in American society have been maintained or increased. I shall return to the prescriptions Lowi and McConnell offer, but first let us examine the model of corporatism developed by comparative research students.

Corporatism

The dream that men might work in harmony to plan their economic and social affairs is not new to comparative politics specialists. As industrialism in Europe crested in the late nineteenth century, thinkers began to envisage a society-wide partnership of dominant social, economic, and political interests. In fact this idea is reflected in National Socialist and Fascist thought in the 1920s and 1930s. Perhaps discredited because of their identification with the German and Italian cause, the various efforts at centralized but not necessarily socialist planning have only recently received serious academic attention (Shonfield 1965; Beer 1969; and Schmitter 1974,

1977). As with pluralism, I shall attempt first to characterize the main elements of the concept. Again I risk simplification, because work on it is only just beginning, and those developing an outline of a theory of corporatism are generally aware of the assumptive, conceptual, and methodological traps outlined earlier (see appendix).

Its principal assumption is the opposite of pluralism: societal-level social and economic planning is possible and necessary. An additional assumption is that such centralized planning is especially appropriate to advanced industrial or postindustrial societies, as they are defined here. Schmitter, the major writer on corporatism, defines the concept thus: "Corporatism can be defined as a system of interest representation in which the constituent units are organized into a limited number of singular compulsory, hierarchically ordered and functionally differentiated categories, recognized or licensed (if not created) by the state and granted a deliberate representational monopoly within their respective categories in exchange for observing certain controls on their selection of leaders and articulation of demands and supports" (1974, p. 98). Schmitter further divides corporatism into two categories relevant to different types of societies: "Societal corporatism appears to be the concomitant, if not ineluctable, component of the postliberal, advanced capitalist, organized democratic welfare state; state corporatism seems to be a defining element of, if not structural necessity for, the antiliberal, delayed capitalist, authoritarian, neomercantilist state" (p. 105). Finally, Panitch argues for the explanatory utility of corporatism for the study of society and politics: "The corporatist paradigm as understood to connote *a political structure within advanced capitalism which integrates organized socioeconomic producer groups through a system of representation and cooperative mutual interaction at the leadership level and of mobilization and social control at the mass level* can be heuristic tools for appropriating the social reality of many Western democracies" (Panitch 1977, p. 66).

The emphasis in corporatism, as captured by the Schmitter quotations, is on hierarchically structured, centralized, functionally differentiated interest groups operating in harmony. This design is clearly in the centralization tradition discussed earlier (chap. 2). However, before critically evaluating this model from the perspective of the argument presented in this book, let us return to the prescriptions of our two critics of pluralism.

Neither Lowi nor McConnell argues for corporatism per se. Both wish to see an end to emphasis on informality in rule making and adjudication. Lowi places his faith in a revived Supreme Court and argues for something he calls "Juridical Democracy." He also advocates restoration of regional government (the nature of which he does not spell out) and a tenure of statutes act, the equivalent of sundown legislation for all agencies. The heart of Lowi's formulation of a cure for the ills of interest-group liberalism rests on the assumption that the American political system can get back on the right track through the formality of law that will enable the public interest to be more closely approximated; his vision, then, is a return to a pluralism safeguarded by a set of guardians in the judiciary. However, Lowi does not deal with the critics of change through the legal system, although typically the legal system favors conservative interests more than the forces of change. McConnell, though writing earlier, presents a more straightforward plea for centralization:

> They [the prescriptions] ask the strengthening of those elements of the political order which tend towards the creation of a constituency of the entire nation. These include the party system, the presidency, and the national government. They also include reassertion of public values and a clearer understanding of the means by which these may be achieved. They involve an acceleration of that evolution of federalism which, however hesitantly, has led toward the building of a nation. They require rejection of the illusions that informality of government produces justice, that political power can be abolished, and that the surrender of public authority to private hands results in democracy. [P. 368]

Is Corporatism the Wave of the Future?

Schmitter (1977) states that pluralism, corporation, and syndicalism are related concepts that can be appropriately used to study western European societies. However, pluralism is really seen by Schmitter as an incipient form of corporatism. Thus it appears reasonable to place pluralism perhaps organizationally subordinate to corporatism.

I shall pass over the important but secondary difficulties of conception and issues of method and technique in the study of corporatism for two reasons. I am not sure that the work on corporatism should be singled out for the same round of criticism leveled at the more familiar models of sociopolitical change because the field is so new; at this point confusion is to be expected over terminology, the nature of subcomponents such as interest-group mediation systems (ibid.), data problems, and whether the concept promises to be more than just another descriptive metaphor. Moreover, the corpus of work on corporatism has already yielded impressive results. For too long comparative specialists ignored the centrality of interest groups in the political process—the focus of American pluralists. The work that was developed (Eckstein 1960; Beer 1969) remained outside the theory-building efforts of the time. And the classification and analysis of interest-group behavior is important in its own right, as such groups constitute the essential ingredients of politics. Post-industrial societies, in which there has been a longer time to develop organized interests, may really be called organizational societies in which little of social-economic or political significance occurs outside labor, management, or political interest groups (Kvavik 1976). Moreover, attention to the relationships between economic and political interests is a welcome addition to the new emphasis on political economy as a subject. What, then, are the objections to the corporatism paradigm?

First, as a society-wide system, corporatism is a form of economic and political organization that rises above the parochial private interests that concern McConnell; smaller interest groups are not only likely to be weaker than large groups but nondemocratic as well, in terms of representation. However, what evidence is there that this larger-group system will solve the representation issue? In fact, other things being equal, from collective action theory we would expect the opposite to be the case (Olson 1965). Two distinct possibilities appear in a large increase in the size of interest groups. One is the common-pool problem graphically described by Hardin (1968). In situations in which each group has no choice but to pursue its own interest, McConnell's fears would be realized. Alternatively, for a variety of internal and external reasons, interest groups might form the coalitions that add up in the end to Schmitter's corporate society (see also Lijphart 1969). In this situation the major interests in society—of which government is only one—combine forces in more or less well developed log-rolling coalitions to reduce political conflict by dividing up resources and engaging in long-range planning. No one, of course, wishes to anticipate the social and political equivalent of Malthus's population prediction. However, let us examine two negative implications of the second alternative. If one—either an interest group or an individual—is outside the corporate system (like the old, the rural and urban poor) one's chances for economic redress, for equality, for gaining any benefits from the organized interest group are remote. Second, once the group system is organized, it becomes the interest of those within it to continue to exclude those outside. This fact will become important when one considers the implications of postindustrial change presented in this book. I have argued that postindustrialization presages changes which renders the corporate vision suspect or fleeting.

The corporate model does not anticipate a wholesale transformation of the existing system of political participation. Its vision really appears most appropriate to that peak point of the industrial phase of change when citizens are relatively satisfied because of full achievement of an adequate-good environment. At this stage basic social institutions and public services have been established, substantial material goods are available, and the changeover to the service sector, with its attached growth in interdependence and externalities, has yet to come.[2] However, as the economy and society move into the postindustrial phase, like other models built on the assumption of the merits of centralization, corporatism declines in relevance. For no longer are citizens so willing to delegate their rights to leaders of established and centralized institutions. It becomes the age of participation, not authority. In such a period—when different goods and services and different-sized government units to deliver them are needed—the cooperation and harmony of the corporate society is shattered. I do not believe corporatism has a place in postindustrial society. What is needed is redesign of political institutions to produce more flexible mixes of decentralized and centralized structures that are useful in a more complicated, information-centered age. As a metaphor, "political ecology" may prove an appropriate term in an age in which man attempts to adjust his institutions in response to a more complex set of political demands about more complicated problems of wants and the instruments to them.

8 Local Government in Postindustrial Britain

A central implication of this work with relevance to public policy concerns the mix of centralization and decentralization in our political institutions; the argument is that one must actually expect diseconomies of scale to result from the centralization of many public institutions. It may eventually be possible to construct more formal and general arguments concerning the optimal design of the size of government institutions appropriate to deliver various types of goods. However, part of the debate is really over epistemological assumptions about relationships of efficiency and size, which makes it difficult to challenge the dominance of the centralization principle. Here I shall look at the centralization/decentralization issue underlying the attempt to reform local government in England.

The study of local government presents problems representative of those found in all fields of political science. One needs data, but aggregate census and fiscal data are collected for purposes other than those intended by the researcher. Surveys are expensive, typically noncomparative, and not repeated. Conceptual issues require attention as well. Local government is concerned with the efficient provision of goods and services required by citizens. How do we define "efficiency"? What is meant by "local government"? What goods and services should be provided? What about the future of local government in postindustrial societies in which citizen demands on governments appear to be unlimited? Is there an optimum balance between participation and authority? Finally, while there are no magic keys to unlock solutions to these issues, the absence of

This chapter is adapted from Roger Benjamin, "Local Government in Postindustrial Britain: Studies of the British Royal Commission on Local Government," pp. 145-72 in *Comparing Urban Service Delivery Systems: Structure and Performance,* ed. Vincent Ostrom and Frances Pennell Bish, Urban Affairs Annual Reviews, vol. 12, © 1977, by permission of the publisher, Sage Publications, Inc.

theory must be identified as the major problem in the study of local government. Without theory, contradictory conclusions and policy recommendations may be reached, sometimes from the same data. The results of ecological and survey studies cannot be evaluated properly because the interpreter does not have a structuring principle from which he may analyze the statistical findings. Such findings have meaning only if they corroborate or contradict hypotheses grounded in deductively generated theory (Brunner and Liepelt 1972).

In this chapter I shall approach these questions through an anatomy of local government reorganization in England. In examining this major set of public policy changes, I shall draw some inferences about the relationship between research and reform in local government by applying lessons from the collective goods approach (Ostrom and Ostrom 1971) and from recent work in the study of comparative political change.

Local Government Reform

In 1972 local government in England was reorganized under the provisions of the Local Government Act (1972) to come into effect in 1974. The act and this analysis deals with local government in England, excluding Scotland and Wales (Wheatley Commission 1969). The act stipulated considerable change in the existing government structure, which had been based on the Local Government Act of 1888. Although the reorganization effected does not entirely follow the recommendations of the Royal Commission on Local Government in England (1969) the arguments and conclusions of the commission (the Redcliffe-Maud report) were largely accepted by the government as guides in their law-making and implementation efforts. These recommendations offer a useful point of departure.

From 1966 to 1969 the commission examined written evidence from government departments and local government associations; received written and oral evidence from 2,156 witnesses, either as private individuals or representatives of professional organizations; carried out a substantial research program of its own; and commissioned a number of studies by independent institutions. Finally, the commission had the benefit of the work of numerous related commissions and government-sponsored studies on welfare, the National Health Service, and local government itself. Perhaps there are government-commissioned studies of comparable magnitude in public policy fields in the United States or elsewhere, but it is difficult to imagine a more extensive study of local government organizations.

The Proposals and Reforms Adopted

The commission found the following structural weaknesses in English local government: (1) fragmentation of government units (79 county boroughs and 45 counties), (2) division of responsibility between upper and lower tiers within counties and between counties and boroughs, (3) the small size of many bodies of authority, with resulting ineffectiveness in dealing with central government and difficulty in recruiting professional staff, (4) an arbitrary division between town and country, and (5) an unsatisfactory relationship between local authorities and the public.

Following these conclusions about local authorities, the Labour government white paper (*Reform of Local Government in England* 1970) suggested that the number of unitary authorities should be reduced from 58 to 51. The Conservative government white paper that followed (*Local Government in England* 1972) argued that because of the competing claims of efficiency (which demanded larger units) and democracy (which demand smaller ones), compromises had to be reached. Tasks were to be divided between two tiers of authority, counties and smaller districts. The allocation of functions was to differ between highly industrialized and rural areas. In conurbations (Standard Metropolitan Areas) effective organization of responsibility of such important services as education and personal social services was felt to require a population base of between 250,000 and 1 million, and therefore it was possible to draw up a compact second tier of metropolitan districts. As area-wide authorities, these metropolitan districts were smaller than counties. In rural areas the second-tier authorities would have to be much smaller in population if they were to be reasonably compact in area. Here primary functions were to remain with the county council. Rural parishes were to continue, while parish councils were to be formed in former boroughs and urban districts.

The Conservative government reorganization has forced county amalgamation and the merger of boroughs with counties. At the county level distinctions between town and country are eliminated. In population, all metropolitan counties exceed 1 million, and the metropolitan districts average 100,000. Functions are divided between two tiers. The top tier has responsibility for functions that are felt to demand more uniformity or greater control by central government. This includes essentially all high-capital investment in nonmetropolitan districts. Metropolitan districts maintain responsibility for education and other social services.

In sum, the 1972 Conservative reorganization follows the spirit and assumptions of the 1969 Redcliffe-Maud report, thus creating another stage in the process of increasing the size of local government and centralizing the functions it performs. The number of top-tier county authorities was reduced to less than 40 percent of the previous total, while the total number of local government units was reduced from just over 1,000 to slightly over 400. The total number of local councillors was reduced to 25,000; the positions of about 11,600 councillors and more than 4,000 aldermen were eliminated. Central government in England retains much greater control over local government than in the United States. Through the legal principle of *ultra vires,* Parliament does not allow local authorities powers not explicitly conferred upon them by statutory authority. Central government also controls local government: government departments supervise the work of local authorities, especially in education, police protection, and urban regional planning.

Questions of optimum local authority size and differentiation of functions between upper- and lower-tier authorities are related to the underlying issue of organizational efficiency. The new government reorganization incorporated the ideas of commissions that worked on related matters throughout the 1960s (Maud Committee 1967; Bains Committee 1972). These commissions all endorse principles of greater staff professionalization, more personnel to fulfill increasingly specialized functions, and the use of modern techniques of management as contributing to increased efficiency.

An Internal Critique

The commission was charged "to consider the structure of Local Government in England, outside Greater London, in relation to its existing functions; and to make recommendations for authorities and boundaries, and for functions and their division, having regard to the size and character of areas in which these can be most effectively exercised and the need to sustain a viable system of local democracy" (*Royal Commission on Local Government in England* 1969, 1:iii; hereafter cited as *Royal Commission*). The commission concluded that England should be divided into 58 unity authorities plus three conurbations, in which authority would be divided between an upper tier responsible for planning, transportation, and development functions and a number of lower-tier metropolitan districts responsible for education, personal social services, health, and housing. The commission further recommended that eight provincial authorities be established with regional planning functions. In addition, local councils were to be encouraged to "represent and communicate the wishes of cities, towns, and villages" (p. 2). Moreover, I note the underlying question which governed commission thinking: "What size of authority or range of size, in terms of population and of area, is needed for the democratic and *efficient* provision of particular services and for local government as a whole?" (p. 3; emphasis added).

The test of the validity of these conclusions and the assumptions upon which they are built rests in an appraisal of the commission's evidence. I have noted the extensive evidence secured by the commission. Not surprisingly, the evidence from government departments supported the unitary principle, which argues for larger units and reduced fragmentation of authority. The arguments run parallel to those assumed by the commission to be correct. Economies of scale would bring the benefits of more and better-trained professional staff; they would reduce costs and facilitate planning in a number of ways. "Government departments left us with the impression that, were it not for democratic considerations, they would really like a system of 30 to 40 all-purpose authorities" (p. 43). The rationalization of linkages between levels of government would lead to greater efficiency of local government operation.

Interpretation of the Evidence

The evidence from the commission's research program presents the reader with puzzling contradictions. The heart of the program was the relationship between size and performance. In language perhaps unacceptable to social scientists, it was concluded that "the over-riding impression which emerges from the three studies by outside bodies and from our own study of staffing is that size cannot statistically be proved to have a very important effect on performance" (p. 58). Yet the report goes on to conclude from this that, "since all the statistics used were necessarily compiled on an existing local authority basis, they could not tell us how a new pattern of authorities might perform" (ibid.). The new structures would differ from the old, so we cannot infer that the same lack of relationship between size and performance would be found to exist in the newly constituted authorities. This extraordinary conclusion suggests the difficulties yet to be overcome in research relevant to public policy. The only thing correct about this portion of the commission's position on size-performance relationship is that it is unwise to suggest that findings from one study can be assumed to hold in a possibly divergent setting. However, all empirical tests of relationships (hypotheses) can ever hope to do is corroborate or contradict hypothesized relationships which stem from prior expectations (a theory or theory notion) about the way variables are related. The commission members should have evaluated the reliability and validity of the specific research studies, of course; but to reject a series of statistically significant findings that all run in the same direction (i.e., that size and performance are not related positively) points to the strength of a priori assumptions by commission members which led them to reject nonsupporting evidence. Faced with such evidence from the statistical studies, the commission simply relied more heavily on the impressions of central government departments and thus went on to reaffirm the assumptions they began with: greater size of local authorities will attract better and more specialized staff. "They also make it possible to achieve a more rational distribution of staff and institutions. Larger administration has the additional advantage of spreading the administrative load more evenly" (p. 59). In the absence of another set of assumptions based on a competing theory about the relationship between size and performance in local government, it appears that the commission groped to affirm the unitary principle whenever and wherever possible.

Two other interesting general conclusions of the commission concern democracy and financial structure. It would be disingenuous to accuse commission members of an antidemocracy bias. The report suggests that they accepted the recommendation of the need for increased participation in local government suggested by the Skeffington (1969) report, and they authorized a full-scale community survey of citizen attitudes toward local authorities (Research Services, Ltd. 1969). The first difficulty, one recognized by the commission, is conceptual: i.e., what are meant by "democracy," "participation," and "community"? The second problem is how to develop operational measures in the domains of related concepts.

Community: What constitutes community in terms relevant to the construction of appropriate local government units? Local government accessibility and responsiveness: To what extent do citizens perceive local government authorities as accessible to them and responsive to their demands? Decentralization: What is the relevance of local councils for greater participation? Representation and community attitudes: To what extent do individual characteristics of electors and elected—e.g., sex, age, length of local residence, education, and respective attitudes toward local government mirror one another, and what are citizen attitudes toward concepts of community in terms of alternative sizes and types of local authority structures?

The community survey found that most citizens tend to identify local community as their home area, no matter what its population size. Though not commented upon directly, the high degree of voter apathy toward local government concerned the commission members as well. When asked whether they preferred a reformed system of local government to the present one, most citizens said they desired the status quo. The commission chose to interpret this as irrelevant, because from their viewpoint most people will indicate a preference for the status quo unless there is very substantial evidence before them indicating the need for change. This may be so, but why? Another view, based on the collective goods approach to be introduced below, is this: citizens will forgo government (or any organizational) change affecting them unless the net benefits of the change are perceived as outweighing the net benefits of the status quo. And, not surprisingly, elected officials are not representative of the citizens they serve in terms of individual characteristics; they tend to be male, older, and better educated than the citizens they serve. No relationship was found between interest in local government and the size of the local authority; apathy toward local government, measured by name recognition of councillors, is apparently distributed equally throughout the local authorities regardless of size.

The difficulty with financial structure concerns the rise in expenditures. The commission contented itself with noting that the steady rise in the proportion of GNP devoted to local government (about 15 percent in 1966-67) must decline at some point in the future (*Royal Commission,* 1:130). One member stated that local government expenditures may rise to 24 percent by the turn of the century

(Senior 1969, p. 148). This seems to me an extraordinary projection given the state of the British economy, even in 1969. A reading of the local government financing projections (*Royal Commission,* 3:95–129) suggests how difficult it would be to keep local government finance on a level with inflation—and all this before the double-digit inflation of the 1970s. Nowhere does one find discussion of how to handle the question of priorities among the social services that local authorities would face when financial growth slowed or stopped (Lapping 1970). Neither did the commission recognize that greater professionalization itself is likely to result in greater costs. Professionalization appears to be associated with more pay, less work, and increasingly liberal retirement programs. The consequence is a function of the stronger bargaining position accruing to those who enjoy a constrained and selective market situation.

Hence the commission recommended unitary authorities that would remove the artificial boundaries between town and country and a minimum "ideal" authority size of approximately 250,000, with 1 million population cited as the upward limit, though in the words of the report (*Royal Commission,* 1:71), "our conclusion is that there is no single service in which administration by a very large authority would have decisive disadvantages. Future developments in most services seem almost certain to favor much bigger operational units than most of the existing ones."[1]

The Senior Dissent

Before turning to an external critique of local government reform in England, I wish to comment on the memorandum of dissent written by commission member Derek Senior (1969), which elaborates on several of my criticisms here. He presents a criticism of the unitary principle, notes the propensity of bureaucrats to select larger minimum population units than necessary, and supports the idea of a local council (he defines it as a "common" council) with political powers rather than one that merely serves a representational function. He correctly interprets the statistical studies not only as denying the hypothesis that economies of scale are associated with size but, in several cases, as indicating *dis*economies of scale associated with size. Instead of a unitary local authority system, Senior recommends a two-tier system organized around a city-region set of counties functionally defined in terms of spatial boundaries isolated by relative densities of population. Senior envisages the common council only where the sense of community is strong enough to demand one.

In one sense, Senior's strategy is superior to the commission recommendation which rigidly prescribes local councils in every borough or county district. However, balanced against the self-organization principle are a series of questions related to resource distribution for the quality of life of both rural and urban inhabitants. D. M. Hill (1973) argues, for example, that local government boundaries may act to perpetuate social-economic inequalities, inequalities which do exist in England (*Royal Commission on the Distribution of Income and Wealth* 1975). Local authorities that organize to develop neighborhood parks, libraries, and other social services may draw a greater than average share of the metropolitan area's resources. Whether, to what extent, and how local government units should be used to redress social-economic inequalities is a complex problem involving conceptions of the ideal polity, social justice, and the effects of various proposed reforms.

Why were Senior's criticisms of the unitary principle and suggestions ignored? One suspects it was because his proposal was not built on a clear theoretical base that would recommend itself strongly enough over the unitary concept so tenaciously held by his colleagues.

Collective Goods and Local Government Reform

The commission recommendations betray confusion over the goals of local government and the theory (or theories) about how it works or, more important, how it might be changed to work better. How might we improve this situation?

I argue below that local government in postindustrial society is increasingly concerned with conflict generated by spillover effects, free-rider problems, and negative externalities created by the continuing growth of government in societies that are reaching new stages of interdependence (LaPorte 1975).

The implications of the collective goods theory for alternative structures of English local government are significant. Though even central ministries indicated ambivalence about the impact of ever increasing centralization of government functions in large public bureaucracies, none of the commission members or witnesses appeared to have before them the structuring principle of public choice that would have allowed them to look at local government in a different light. Let us look again at the two basic problems considered by the commission.

Size and Efficiency of Local Authorities

The commission members, with the exception of Senior, adhered to the view that size and efficiency are correlated in a linear manner; the greater the size, the greater the level of efficiency. Of course the commission is in good company; this view is dominant among students and practitioners of local government (cf. Ostrom 1972). Greater size is assumed to lead to the achievement of a "critical mass," defined as the existence of an organization large enough to allow sufficient specialization to perform the function relevant to its organizational goals competently. It is also felt that greater size promotes economies of scale. One single-purpose educational bureaucracy can purchase equipment less expensively than a number of smaller educational authorities. However, the collective goods approach suggests a different view of the probable effects of size on efficiency,[2] which alerts us to the likelihood that beyond a certain size, inefficiencies will result.

This different perspective gives us an alternative set of expectations concerning the findings of the commission. Though the commission studies do not lend support to the anticipated positive relationship between size and efficiency, inspection of the two best-designed studies, relying on econometric techniques, corroborates the interpretation based on collective goods. For example, with respect to housing, the York study concludes, "Considering 'cost per foot' as the relevant dependent variable, our findings for the County Boroughs suggest the opposite of what has been the common view about the effect of an increase in the population or 'size' of a local authority on its efficiency. . . . Diseconomies of scale operate with an increase in the population size" (Gupta and Hutton 1968, p. 6). With respect to another measure, management costs per dwelling unit, the study concludes that for noncounty boroughs and rural district councils the hypothesis concerning economies of scale is refuted. And for urban district councils, "our findings suggest a U-shaped supervision and management cost curve with relation to population, such costs being kept at their minimum when the population size of an Urban District Council is about 40,000, beyond which tending to rise. Therefore, an increase in their size beyond

40,000 would also give rise to diseconomies of scale" (ibid., p. 7). The York study authors find the same U-shaped curve for cost and population for health care measures and another inverse curve for size of population of authorities and the expenditure per mile of highway construction.

The second study examines the relationship between performance and size of local educational authorities. The authors of this study, also using regression analysis of expenditure data, find that larger authorities spend more on texts than small authorities (Local Government Operational Research Unit 1968, p. 40) and that the cost of maintenance and replacement of educational equipment increases sharply with the size of the population being served by the authority. In addition, larger authorities appear to have fewer, rather than proportionally more, specialist advisers than their smaller counterparts; there is an increase in expenditures for specialists and advisers from the very small to medium-sized authorities but a decline in expenditures after that point (ibid., p. 112).

The Need to Differentiate among Public Goods

Most commission members distinguished between the size and type of government institution required by intensive face-to-face social services and those more appropriate to larger administrative units such as water or sewage services. A return to the discussion of collective goods (chap. 2) suggests why it is important to differentiate among public goods. There, I noted the importance of distinguishing goods that are information-sensitive from those goods that are not. Moreover, without careful planning, nonresidents may gain significant free-rider benefits while citizens who are actually paying for services may not be able to enjoy them.

When we bring to bear our model of government and collective goods in postindustrial societies, several points become clear. In addition to evidence concerning the growth of negative externalities associated with the legacy of industrialization, there are data to suggest that one major economic feature of postindustrial society is concern for equity in the distribution of wealth, not its growth. Though research on this problem is just beginning, it may be that, after a minimum welfare level is achieved in industrialized societies, economic inequalities between classes do not decline (*Royal Commission on Distribution of Income and Wealth* 1975). Hirschman (Hirschman and Rothschild 1973) argues that if economic growth is not followed by substantial redistribution of wealth, class conflict will increase. This conflict may be deferred in a relatively homogeneous society, because citizens will hold the expectation that they will eventually share in economic growth. However, when they perceive that this expectation is not likely to be fulfilled, their response by way of strikes, demonstrations, or other forms of political demands will be even more intense. England, the oldest industrialized society, has had the greatest amount of time to generate economic growth and achieve economic equality. If it is correct that social-economic inequality there has remained relatively constant for decades (*Royal Commission on the Distribution of Income and Wealth* 1975) working-class militancy and high-level demands on government find a possible explanation in the Hirschman model.[3]

There are studies to draw on with respect to the social and cultural change linked with postindustrialization, including Inglehart's (1971) paper showing that since 1945 younger people appear to be increasingly freed of material needs and are adopting "postbourgeois" values of intellectual and aesthetic need and "belongingness." This is true of the middle and upper classes, but workers' values, especially those of older workers, remain dominated by the need to protect their material and physical security. In politics Inglehart conceives of the value change as resulting in preferences for participation in decision making and protection of freedom of speech versus bourgeois preferences for the maintenance of order and protection against inflation. The preference for political participation over authority maintenance finds echoes in studies of English local government, the commission report itself, and cross-national studies. The question is why, and what are the consequences of this preference for local government?

Industrialization in England brought many benefits. One could give a roll call of domestic increases in the quality of life as well as citing international triumphs. However, after a time spillover effects of industrialization began to mount. A centralized government sufficiently large to function in an industrialized era becomes over-institutionalized (Kesselman 1970) in the postindustrial period. Its large bureaucracies become increasingly ill adapted to the growing and differentiated needs of the public they serve. The growth of citizen demand is brought on by spillover effects throughout society, which require public solutions, plus the change in individual preference schedules: acceptance of the mere existence of services yields to a demand for increased quality of performance and eradication of existing inequalities (Brittan 1975). At the individual level, the change in the content of preference schedules may be assumed to be a rational response to fundamental changes in the social-economic level of development.

In England, as in other western European societies, alternative-education groups desire basic reforms in the nature, not the provision, of education. Neighborhood groups organize to fight negative externalities such as noise and air pollution or new highway construction and attempt to create higher-quality local environments. These collective action units are spurred on by the environment in which they operate.

This sketch is simply an outline of a plausible explanation for the growth in participation demands in England; the research remains to be done. In retrospect, we should not be surprised that the kinds of government appropriate to one era might need adjustment, a shift in emphasis, or wholesale replacement in another period. When flexible responses are required to meet diverse wants, the previous highly centralized political institutions are unlikely to be appropriate if public choice-based notions about the relationship between size and efficiency are correct. An increase in public goods and externalities can add up to increased divisiveness and conflict.

To return to the commission report, the commission's emphasis on local participation provides support for my explanatory sketch. Assuming that further social-economic change in England will continue in the postindustrial direction, additional danger signals are found in recent studies. In a follow-up to Inglehart's (1971) study, Marsh (1975) presents evidence of a continuing increase in the percentage of Englishmen with postbourgeois values. Marsh divided his sample into two groups, acquisitive (materialist) and postbourgeois. Whereas 9 percent of the acquisitive group indicated dissatisfaction with the district in which they lived, 21 percent of the postbourgeois group expressed discontent. In addition, the postbourgeois group were dissatisfied with the "unresponsiveness of elected representatives toward the electorate and more dissatisfied with the level of democracy in Britain" (p. 25). While the total economy has been growing slowly or experiencing negative growth, the local government share of GNP rose from 13.8 percent in 1964 to 15.4 percent in 1974. The burden of interest and debt payment on local government has increased greatly in the past few years, and yet demands on government at all levels, appears inexhaustible (King 1975).

Conclusion

In comparison with the United States (Banfield 1960), pressure on local government in England has not been great. Only recently, for example, has the number of automobiles reached the absorption capacity of the road network. Social welfare case loads do not approach American levels, and crime rates, though rising, are also very small in comparison with those in the United States. Yet pressure on local government has begun to intensify rapidly in recent years. Throughout the 1960s the proportion of Britain's GNP devoted to the public sector increased enormously. While local government autonomy had been small, the reorganization efforts of the past few years have resulted in even greater centralization—this in spite of the contradictory evidence discussed here. There are several implications in all this.

Finance. The commission's mandate did not include consideration of local government finance. This was a serious omission. On the surface, English local authorities such as the Greater London Council appear to be in better financial condition than, say, New York City, but this is only appearance. Most American local governments are prevented by statute from spending beyond set limits. Most of the operating revenues for English local authorities come from central government, so there is no immediate danger of "bankruptcy"; but there, as in other postindustrial societies, inflation and the slowdown in the rate of increase in GNP is likely to result in substantial financial deterioration of the entire public sector in the next decade (Lapping 1970).

Political participation. I have argued that the rise in participation demands is not a time-honored but otherwise meaningless plea for more democracy. It stems from two perspectives that are converging rapidly. First, the rise in spillover effects may tend to reinforce existing levels of economic and social inequalities through government's failure to ameliorate those problems. These spillovers occur not only because of the effects of private industry but because government is so heavily involved in providing essentially "mixed" goods, which in turn create the need for local responses. Second, as individuals become better educated, have more leisure, and are more free of material needs, they and their collectives unite to demand differential treatment from large, anonymous bureaucracies which find it difficult to respond to particular preferences of smaller groups of citizens. The growth of diverse wants may in fact be what postindustrialization is all about.

The future is likely to bring unpleasant surprises to adherents of the unitary principle of government. "Hidden hand" modeling by operations research analysts conceals biases as broad and skewed as any other style of planning (Downs 1969). There is no way I know of to gauge the preferences of individuals correctly without allowing them an opportunity to express such preferences. Cost-benefit calculations can be made concerning the consequences of many issues, but this action fails to take into account the diversity of various preferences and the intensity with which they are held. Here Ostrom's suggestions for institutional redesign are useful.[4] His concept of polycentricity captures the need for autonomous but overlapping catchments in postindustrial societies.

Suggestions

I would proceed upon the following principles. First, it is important to design local authorities and public bureaucracies to fulfill single and multipurpose functions within a representative community base defined along the lines suggested by the Senior (1969) dissents. In this connection, principles emanating from the criticism presented above should be implemented. Since public goods delivered by government differ, so should the government units designed to deliver them. For example, a legal authority spread over a wide geographic area and cutting horizontally across many government units may be appropriate for dealing with the Thames tidal basin; however, small government units, with their labor-intensive aspect, appear more suitable for implementing the imperatives of the Royal Commission on Local Government to coordinate personal social services to the needs of the individual and the family. In this respect the two-tier division of responsibilities makes matters worse. Although the two-tier notion is essentially a principle developed in recognition of the differences in types of public goods, the power-sharing arrangements discussed (Jones 1973, pp. 154–55) only create more uncertainty and delay arising from communication difficulties and misunderstanding about responsibilities. A better strategy would be to give local authorities and particular public corporations maximum legal powers consistent with their ability to carry out their functions. This would include taxation powers whenever possible.

Postindustrial society brings new problems to local government, and fundamental alteration of its design and of demands placed upon it is not far off. The main reason unitary-based local government worked in the past very likely was the light burdens placed on it until the past decade. In any case, in the 1970s the problems encountered in English urban and rural life begin to sound distressingly similar to those of North America's big cities: rising crime rates, minority problems, traffic and pollution issues. The unitary approach to local government, which has had more currency in England because of the historical propensity of its citizens to allow elites wide latitude in government (Schwartz and Wade 1972), has been questioned in this chapter. Perhaps it is time to begin to think in terms of political ecology rather than the political development of local government, just as ecology—the qualitative management of finite human and economic resources—is becoming substituted for growth.

9 The Problem of Political Design

Kumar (1976) criticizes correctly the tendencies of writers on postindustrialization to ascribe a large degree of autonomy to the political system. If the discussion presented here has merit, a number of plausible projections can be made about political change in postindustrial societies. Here I shall consider only three: (1) the political implications of the service sector; (2) the rise and changing nature of political conflict; and (3) the case for institutional redesign. Much of the structural change in postindustrialization offers little other choice to political elites than to redesign political institutions; however, how they are redesigned is another matter.

There are both obvious and more subtle points to be made about the service sector concept, an idea that masks subcategories that should be more distinctively highlighted. First, resort to collective action through unionization is occurring among all elements of the service sector, and this trend will continue. Because of its size relative to industry and agriculture, as time passes, activities in the service sector will take on added significance (Fuchs 1968; Holmes 1966; Hartwell 1971; and Bell 1973). Regardless of whether one foresees political chaos (Huntington 1974), or a happy politics of postscarcity (Bell 1973), the service sector will surely play the major role in deciding which or what combination of these futures will prevail. However, in order to assess the political impact of the service sector, much work needs to be done to differentiate the categories lumped together under the general heading of "service." The main distinction I would make is based on Baumol's discrimination of technically progressive and nonprogressive economic activities. I would suggest at least three kinds of service sector divisions.[1] First, I would place together all technically progressive areas. It is important to distinguish those economic activities such as information-related sciences that are capable of successive iterations of improvement (measured in quantitative productive terms) and that also provide the engine to drive innumerable technical adaptations, many of which are counted in the industrial sector itself. Second, there are a wide range of private service functions that, as I argued in chapter 3, make man's life qualitatively better but are more difficult to measure progress in. These are virtually limitless—they include from floor sanding and home decorating, window washing and furniture repair. But while it is difficult to measure progress in the areas being served, eliminating these functions from prominent consideration would be a questionable action. Third, I would group public service activities together and make subdivisions within the group. Services in the public sector may be divided into public and quasi-public (or collective) goods. As I argued in chapter 2, we have no easy method of deciding which of these goods should be provided. However, one plausible inference can be made: there may be upper limits to the public sector, at least in liberal democracies, and we may be near these limits. The problem is that we have no standards by which to judge when the limits are reached. In societies such as Britain the welfare state is being selectively dismantled as Conservative and Labour governments attempt to work within the constraints of a declining industrial base and rising inflation. If in fact we are warranted in assuming natural upper limits to the public sector (or, alternatively, to particular welfare expenditures), the case for redesign of political institutions is strengthened. We shall be forced to consider which services are essential, which can be handled by private firms or volunteer action, and which can be dispensed with altogether. The idea of a national service, reintroduced by Dahrendorf (1975) among others, is useful. Useful too are suggestions concerning the viability of a return to the local community functions currently being fulfilled by regional and central government units. This is so because, if postindustrialization is marked by a threshold rise in interdependence, concern for qualitative reorganization of man's institutions, equality, and hence an increase in collective goods, our twentieth-century emphasis on centralization in political design will decline. The present mosaic of political institutions will inevitably become a new design. It is up to man to grasp the leadership opportunity afforded by the design necessities.

In sum, we may expect the political impact of the service sector to be greater than that of industry; the position of industry will come to be analogous to agriculture—small as a proportion of the total work force and GNP but privileged because of its crucial contribution to the economy. Unionization of public employees is already more or less advanced, depending on the country in question, and we should expect this trend to continue. Privileges and status gained are not easily given up, and we may expect a considerable rise in public demands and strikes as the economic burden becomes unbearable for the state. Equally difficult to deal with are the quantitative as well as qualitative issues associated with the provision of public and quasi-public goods. In postindustrial societies the question of how much of a good to supply is often more salient than whether to supply the good in the first place. Debates over how much public money is sufficient for health is only one example. Despite substantial increases in funds for public education in the United States, there is reason to believe that reading and mathematics levels attained in previous decades in this country are declining. The same problem occurs in the areas of crime, social welfare, and housing policy. There are two points to be made about this issue. The minor point is that indeed, additional capital investments in human services provided by the state may be reaching a point of diminishing returns. And this takes on added significance if upper limits to public expenditures are being approached. More important, if postindustrialization does involve the slowdown of growth and a renewed concern for quality, we may be nearing the peak in the curves measuring the pathological correlates of industrialization. Many social observers see the community breakdown that accompanies the industrialization process—a breakdown itself exacerbated by the rapidity of the social-economic change—as the underlying cause of increases in crime, disruption of the family, mental illness, etc. In the postindustrial process-state man may again have the time necessary to renew community bonds (perhaps in new forms) that promote the stability of interpersonal relationships, as well as a greater sense of spatial and temporal familiarity—all of which may serve to develop a renewed sense of community that would obviate much of the artificial patchwork of the welfare state. I shall return to this point below, but first it is important to place the service sector in the context of a new type and level of political conflict that also serves to promote the case for institutional redesign.

It is critical at the outset to define the concept of political conflict because the term carries ambiguities. Here we may array political participation along a continuum and distinguish nonroutine demand-making activities. This category may include significant new interest-group demands on political authority, work slowdowns, strikes and demonstrations, and low and high levels of political violence. Earlier I noted macro-level structural changes which I believe presage (*a*) a rise in political conflict and (*b*) the changing nature of that conflict. I shall discuss these issues in turn.

First, Hibbs (1976) has modeled the rise in industrial conflict in approximately the same set of societies that form the empirical base of this study. Far from declining, as predicted by end-of-ideology scenarios in the late 1950s, strike activity has either remained constant or increased. Hibbs's findings are consistent with Inglehart's (1971) revolution in values thesis and can be plausibly if discomfitingly interpreted by the model I have presented in chapter 2. If, because of the presence of the image of adequate good, individual values for many are being transformed from concern for material wants to social-psychological desires, the growing documentation of anomie and despair on the factory floor find a plausible interpretation. The psychological costs of meaningless assembly line work quickly escalate when an adequate goods environment is assured. Indeed many schemes—such as worker-management power sharing, the return to group-oriented total product assembly being tried in Sweden, and the continuing automation of many assembly line jobs—all make sense. Provided that man can profit from the leisure time gained (Scitovsky 1976), the postindustrial process-state may be the phase in which man comes a little closer to the liberation from machines envisaged by Comte, Saint-Simon, and Marx himself. Thus the portion of worker-based rise in political conflict that is a result of man's urge to be free of such labor should be greeted as a positive force. Unfortunately, I must add that little thought has been devoted to the equally severe psychological stress placed on many service and especially public workers. It is true that most of these workers are far from the noise and dirt of the shop floor, but they are surrounded by the sort of visual boredom evoked by the United States government interior greens, numbed by Muzak, deprived of reasonable levels of human interaction, and consigned to work routines devoid of novelty. Only the types, not the degree, of illness differ between white- and blue-collar workers. Disregarding the possibility that the nature of white-collar bureaucratic work leaves man less able to respond critically than blue-collar activity, because of the mentally rather than physically exhausting effects of such labor, we may expect a rise in collective action in the service sector as citizens begin to challenge the designs associated with their work life.

As important as these social-psychological incentives are defense-related incentives, compelling radical worker action, that will also increase considerably in our postindustrial process-state. This is true for several reasons. First, I have argued that postindustrialization involves the slowdown of economic growth; increasing inflation may well be a characteristic of such societies until new criteria for productivity are developed. In such a circumstance, the *overall* economy takes on the ominous appearance of a common-pool problem. Success in merely maintaining one's relative economic position then becomes dependent more and more on collective action strength than on demonstrated productivity improvements. And the more central the economic activity, the greater the bargaining power a union or professional group will have.[2] It is not easy to be sanguine about such a state of affairs. The problem may be accentuated in the industrial sector of postindustrial societies, which may become an economic albatross. However, *as long as the basic framework of the nation-state system obtains,* some industrial output will be considered necessary to ensure the integrity of the state. This will be so even when the economic activity in question has lost its comparative advantage in the face of mounting competition from societies moving into industrialization. Thus there will continue to be joint industry-wide efforts to maintain preference—in fact, to enjoy a quasi-public good—at the expense of Pareto-efficient economic criteria. It will not be easy for postindustrial government, however designed, to cope with such issues.

The importance of inequality has also been noted. Postindustrialization may be the era in which man is no longer willing to tolerate the levels of economic and social inequality that, as I have noted, may not have declined during industrialization. This is a problem neither more nor less easily dealt with than the difficulties presented by the emphasis on liberty during periods of maximum economic growth in the industrialization phases of our new postindustrial countries. If, as most contemporary political philosophers agree, classic liberalism during eighteenth- and nineteenth-century American and European industrialization overemphasized liberty at the expense of equality, the drive for total equality in all areas of social as well as economic and political life may be the harbinger of postindustrialization.[3]

I would add here that many of the implications of the growth of postindustrialization in any society run counter to or inhibit the efforts of groups that may still be struggling to achieve an environment supportive of the adequate-good image. The larger the society, the more this is apt to be the case; it is less true of Scandinavian countries than of the United States, with its large black, American Indian, and Chicano groups. The decline of economic growth and the growth of the service sector, with the emerging centrality of information-generating, receiving, and processing skills, doubly frustrates the efforts of many groups to achieve even the minimum level necessary for the existence of the adequate-good image (see Partch 1976 for within-system variation in postindustrial growth).

I have noted the continuing increase of interdependence of all parts of society, which requires constant efforts to calibrate those various elements into harmonious systems (in the words of a Bell Telephone commercial, "the system is the answer"). But in the absence of a sudden development of omniscience, I also suggested the growth of negative externalities that accompanies this growing interdependence, as citizens attempt to control access to themselves while at the same time they are given incentives to resort to collective action to press their own claims on government for particular quasi-public goods. All this results in a growth of political demands that places an overload on existing political institutions. And if the prediction of a rise in positional goods is also accurate, we have the final element that portends a sharp rise in political conflict. For positional goods are by definition zero-sum goods about which conflict, however defined, is inevitable. The greater the number of citizens assured an adequate goods environment, the greater their competition for positional goods.

In sum, the case for institutional reform in political institutions is compelling. Public expenditure limits will force a decline in the provision of some goods provided by government and a restructure of the delivery of many other goods. Citizens' growing propensity to voice complaints (Hirschman and Rothschild 1973) about the quality of the increasingly information-sensitive goods being delivered suggests a need for more decentralized and autonomous government units that can be made more accountable to the fewer and more homogeneous clients in the catchment organized. I have noted the several reasons to expect a rise in political conflict and a related decline of legitimacy in postindustrial political institutions. Indeed, the political world envisaged here is sharply distinct from the apolitical world pictured by Bell (1973) or the corporatist vision of political harmony (Schmitter 1974, 1977). Is Huntington's (1974) pessimistic view appropriate—a decline in central political institutionalization and a rise in inchoate political participation demands: in short, political chaos? I think not, and I end this discussion with my own projections.[4]

First, the nature and meaning of political conflict itself is transformed in postindustrial societies. Quantitatively smaller industrial or service-based strikes will occur. In an interdependent world, the threat of a strike becomes as significant as the strike itself. Moreover, it becomes more difficult for government officials to deny claims based on equality when equality is the dominant political norm. However, the larger point is really simply that conflict about issues concerning the quality of life represents an advance over conflict about conditions that only make life bearable. This is not to say that conflict about positional goods is any less real to citizens than conflict about decent wages or the right to social welfare and health protection; it is simply different. And if we understand *why* change in the design of political institutions is necessary, we can begin to respond positively to that need with alternative institutional designs instead of simply lamenting the decline in authority and effectiveness of political institutions that were conceived and developed for previous process-states.

Toward a Political Ecology

Ours is not the first generation to grapple with the need to find a common ground for claims of equality and liberty; exactly what composes justice changes, at least in part, with man's cognitive orientations across the development process. But what positive inferences and projections can be made?

Recall my argument regarding the slowdown of growth. If the nature of the economy changes, what are some of the effects of this change? Perhaps the largest task may be redefinition of the economy itself. If productivity criteria associated with the industrial era and its manufacturing sector are no longer appropriate, we shall have to derive new evaluative criteria. To some extent this is happening already. In Britain, for example, there is a central pay-policy research unit in government that seeks to establish public and private equivalencies between jobs and pay. Moreover, there exists in Britain a rough pecking order of types of employment, and individual groups keep their place in it through the threat of strikes; when groups do strike, it is often over an alteration of the income differential between themselves and other groups. Public employees, who include university lecturers and doctors, are allocated salaries on the basis of a general societal agreement as to their proper place. The point is that if economic growth slows, this gives economic and political institutions the luxury of more time to deal with the problem of reward criteria in a mainly nonindustrial economy. Equally important is the declining relevance of the assumption of linear economic change in individual production and consumption habits. By definition, the postindustrial economy assumes an adequate-good environment. In addition to the decline of economic growth, the growth of information as a primary descriptive feature alters the meaning of economic change. From our perspective of individual choice, quantitative concern for an increase in income and material status is replaced by a focus on personal experiences that enhance the quality of life, on work and education that lead to increased qualitative differentiation over the entire period of one's life. Thus growth in organized complexity of experience in all dimensions of life becomes the goal—also the dominant societal norm. Second, whereas the predominant concern during industrialization is with such things as alienation in the work place, industrial conflict, and problems of management and productivity, primary attention in postindustrial societies turns to the significance of the service sector. If there is general recognition of the centrality of the service sector, some of the issues associated with it will receive more attention.

The social changes discussed in this book also suggest a number of other possibilities. If population growth declines until a stable population base is achieved; if geographic mobility declines, in terms of urban, suburban, and regional immigration and emigration; if economic growth slows down, man may again have the stability of social-economic ingredients necessary to maintain or, in this case, to reestablish community. Without this slowdown of the rate of change itself, it is difficult to be sanguine about social systems and their communities that virtually disintegrate as the economy passes the peak of industrialization.[5] Moreover, if value change is occurring in the direction suggested by Inglehart (1971, 1977*b*), the changes discussed may lead to greater tolerance of the opinions and values of others, and there may be positive consequences here as well.

We may now add some plausible points to the political changes projected above. First, if there is more social stability and a return to a greater sense of community, this may lead to a decline in demands for government provision of social services. If the pace of change is slower, this may make redundant what are essentially artificial government efforts to recreate community or limit the psychological damage due to its absence. If economic growth slows but the adequate-good image remains, political debate may be more concerned with the qualitative factors of existence than with the presence or absence of material commodities. And the nature of this conflict may itself change; we may still have revolutionary sentiments and revolution itself, but these may be of a redefined sort, lacking a component of physical violence. If the pace of change slows, and demands for government provision of new collective goods slow with it (in any event, demands for collective goods must have an upper limit, even if it is 100 percent), "natural limits"—in a horizontal as well as a vertical sense—of the provision of the varieties of public goods may be reached. Also, a closer approximation of the optimal provision of the various classes of goods may develop; one reason is, again, the presence of time and greater stability of known preferences through information systems developed and then institutionalized.

Conclusion

I end with a series of suggestions and questions, for it would not be profitable to summarize an argument which is itself an agenda for thinking about the nature and direction of research about comparative political change. I shall stress the implications of my main points. First, if there is a set of socioeconomic thresholds beyond which industrialization and its concomitant features begin to slow and are replaced by postindustrialization, at a minimum quantitatively based work on political development must be reassessed. Most such studies make linear assumptions about growth and change when curvilinear assumptions are more appropriate. Second, there is a range of topics and data needs most of which should be collected at the micro (within-nation) level. For example, with better time-series data, more model tuning with polynomial and other curve-fitting techniques can be applied. However, the theoretical and policy issues raised are perhaps the most interesting. There are a number of comments to be made concerning problems related to my argument, in comparative research, theory, method, technique, and data-analysis strategies.

Foremost are the insights brought to related questions by the research program begun here. First, corroboration of the presence of the postindustrial process-state as modeled here reinforces the philosophical and social debate that is beginning on questions of legitimacy (Habermas 1975), rationality, and work (O'Toole 1974; and Habermas 1970) in societies beyond industrialization (Israel 1974). It may in fact be "rational" no longer to accept the sort of "rational" behavior attributed to citizens in industrial societies; examples of "right conduct" in such societies include deference to authority, the subordination of the individual to the "system," etc.

Second, economists such as Galbraith point to the primacy of large corporations, both domestic and multinational, in modern capitalist societies.[6] Concentration of enormous amounts of capital for investment purposes and control of information networks critical to economic decision making are two reasons for corporate power. Yet the argument presented in this book would lead one to question this view. It may well be the case that the only "growth" portion of postindustrial economies will be public rather than industrial or even service. If this is so, the economic basis for the power of corporations will erode. At a minimum, new relationships of government and economy should be anticipated.

Third, there is concern among political party specialists and journalists that the party system may be in an age of decline in western Europe and the United States. Voter turnout continues to decline; citizen expectations about the party system are disappointed; party identification itself is apparently waning, even in the United States, where it has been assumed to be the strongest. These assertions find a plausible explanation here. Collective action based on single issues rises, and continuity, which is needed to maintain effective recruitment channels for political leadership, declines. It may well be difficult for parties to abort the multiplicity of rising political demands that occur as a function of the growth in externalities and other problems of size and efficiency. Thus the relationship of the party system, political participation, and political institutionalization will take on added significance in coming decades (see Huntington 1974).

Fourth, the fundamental thrust of my argument offers a basis for admonitions and suggestions to those societies at earlier stages of political development. There is not only no "end" to development but no guarantee that the paths taken by specific societies in the postindustrial process-state will result in positive arrangements for governance; varieties of politics up to and including revolution—a redefined version thereof—appear possible (McCaughrin 1976). Moreover, the "discovery" of a new process-state places previous process-states in a new light. For example, whereas governments of societies that modernized in the past (pre-World War II) concentrated primarily on the development of national infrastructure and the capacity to deliver basic pure public goods such as national defense and law and order, contemporary governments in new states face demands from their citizens for welfare, service, and other costly goods—demands that are difficult to meet. In addition, new states may profit from alternative development models rather than those based on currently "developed" (postindustrial) societies, which generated environmental problems, high levels of social and economic inequality, and expansionist foreign policies (Dunn 1976). Fifth, let us reconceive political leadership in terms of institutional design opportunities. Thus at thresholds like the transition from an industrial to a postindustrial process-state, innovative political entrepreneurs are needed to create new systems of political institutions or renovate old ones.[7] Within the societies that have moved beyond industrialization, elites that are more maintenance oriented are probably dominant.

I will not restate the basic implication of this book concerning the need for redesign of government institutions. However, two additional points need to be highlighted. First, fiscal equivalence (meaning that beneficiaries bear the cost of efforts to produce benefits) is clearly not the only criterion we wish to apply concerning whether government should deliver goods. Even though we continue without a general social welfare function (Baumol 1969), few would wish to return to a libertarian laissez-faire state. We shall wish to continue to extend social services to disadvantaged sectors of society; the literature on postindustrialization suggests the importance of equity, of distribution questions. Furthermore, if those who feel there are upper limits to public spending are correct (Dahrendorf 1975), at the very least imperatives exist to save essential public services.

Postscript: Is More or Less Government the Issue?

The model presented in this book is also useful for framing a related public policy debate. Scholars labeled neo-conservatives and liberal-socialists note the declining capacity of the state in Western democracies to govern; the phrase "crisis of the state" is often used as a general label.[1] Although the two schools agree that there is a crisis of governance, their solutions to the crisis are diametrically opposed. The neo-conservative argument, within which I shall include studies of government strain and overload, calls for lowered citizen expectations, less political participation, and at least a partial dismantling of government social services. Scholars in the other tradition reach the conclusion that more participation, more government involvement in and delivery of social services, and indeed greater centralization of government provide the answer. I shall argue that both schools have arrived at inappropriate conclusions because they have not grasped the essential qualities of the political impact of social-economic change beyond "development."

The Crisis of the State and Two Solutions

It would not be useful to describe in detail additional reports concerning the crisis of the state. The qualitative evidence is in the form of reports of government paralysis and breakdown, decline of parliaments, failure to stem inflation (e.g., the failure of wage and income policies that have been tried in most countries in the West), and acknowledgment by many political elites and serious political commentators of a paucity of fresh ideas to handle (*a*) unemployment and inflation and (*b*) the growth of political demands, fiscal or otherwise, on government.

The quantitative evidence is in the form of survey research and strike, interest group, unemployment, and fiscal data that reaffirm the same conclusions about the state in the societies in our group (see, e.g., Inglehart 1977*a*; Hibbs 1976; Brittan 1977; and Tufte 1978). The list is formidable: there exist

1. a decline in citizen trust in government;
2. a possible decline in partisanship and thus an erosion of the traditional elite-mass linkage supplied by the political party system;
3. evidence of a substantial increase in the number and type of local-action interest groups;
4. an increase in the number of strikes and their duration;
5. a rise in *both* inflation and unemployment;
6. a greater level of voter fluctuation and cabinet and government turnover; and
7. an increasing inability of central governments to get their proposals accepted: e.g., for nuclear projects, electric power projects, and roads.

The point of interest is that both neo-conservatives and liberal-socialists agree about most aspects of this list. There is one further issue upon which they agree. Their debate is framed by a shared positive association concerning the perceived benefits of centralization over decentralization solutions to institutional problems (Huntington 1968; Deutsch 1963; Schmitter 1977; O'Connor 1973; Harrington 1976; and Ollman 1976).

The Overload School

This group is symbolized by the work of Huntington, Bell, Moynihan, and Kristol in the United States and King, Rose, and Winkler in Britain.[2] Scholars in this group consider a number of specific problems. Though they focus differently, on participation, inflation, increased political demands, etc., they do agree that the appropriate direction for solutions to the crisis in governance is to reduce burdens on government (King 1975), lower expectations (Bell 1975), reduce government services in order to reduce government costs (Rose and Peters 1978), or reduce political participation itself.

The following statement suggests the tenor of this group's concerns: "The tensions likely to prevail in a postindustrial society will probably require a more authoritative and effective pattern of governmental decision-making. The trends in terms of values, ideology, and participation may, however, make authoritative allocation of resources by government more rather than less difficult" (Huntington 1974, p. 160). Huntington argues, subsequently (1975) that the only way to make government work is to lower the increasingly nonregular political participation actions, e.g., the efforts of civic action groups, demonstrations, strikes, and lawsuits.

The consensus of this school is that in order to save or restore central political institutions to their previous levels of institutionalization, governmental burdens must be lowered. If political institutions are not given respite, if citizen expectations are not lowered (Bell 1975), if wage demands, especially in the public sector (Brittan 1975), are not held down, if citizen action groups do not moderate their xenophobic hostility to government energy and other public works, the political future of Western societies is bleak.

The Neo-Marxist School

Liberal-socialist thinkers often describe the same problems and yet reach very different solutions. For example, Kelly, Stunkel, and Wescott argue that postindustrial society will be a world beset by resource scarcity, conflict resulting from population crowding, and general economic decline. Under such conditions, "centralized government and economic planning and administration will be a necessity" (1976, p. 276). O'Connor (1973) sees the state as no longer able to shore up the private sector, and others argue that only an entire state takeover of all economic activities will solve the crisis (Wright 1976). Heilbroner (1977) argues, similarly, that we need much greater government authority in capitalist societies to solve political and cultural as well as economic problems. Etzioni (1977–78) agrees that demands on government have sharply escalated but also argues that the capacity and scope of government authority must be substantially increased and centralized.

Conclusion

The implications of my argument lead one to reject the solution of both schools. I have argued that the notion that government burdens can and must be reduced is naive or outmoded in the face of the structural changes occurring in postindustrial societies. Political demands, political conflict, the age of participation are more than just ideological phrases; they result from fundamental social-economic and political change.

If we cannot expect government burdens to be lowered, what about the appeal for greater centralization of authority as a solution? In one sense, there is more government because there is more and more provision by the public sector of goods like education that were once supplied mainly by the private sector. However, the issue as presented above is whether larger and more centralized government units will resolve some of the problems relating to the crisis of the state.

The answer should, I think, be clear; other things being equal, increased centralization of political institutions will bring more, not fewer, diseconomies of scale.

Appendix: Strategy, Methodology, and Theory Development in Comparative Research

In comparative research there is major confusion over the relationship of strategy, method, and theory development. I shall argue here that the claim for a special "comparative" methodology is unfounded and really represents strategy debates about which dimension—data analysis, concept information, measurement, theory development, or problem formulation—to accent in research. If the "comparative" method does not unite comparativists, what does? I shall attempt to show that acceptance of the assumption of common processes of sociopolitical change arrayed along multiple-continua cross-systems binds those engaged in comparative research and actually suggests a line of defense for it. Finally, in order to justify the research strategy I have undertaken here, I shall evaluate the yield of past efforts in political development (here called sociopolitical change) studies. The evaluation suggests principles of analysis to be followed.

Comparative Research, the "Comparative" Method, and Sociopolitical Change Theory Construction

In a recent issue (vol. 8, July 1975), *Comparative Political Studies* presented a symposium on methodology that touched on most of the critical issues facing comparativists (papers of interest include those of Meckstroth, Lijphart, and Teune). Aided by the points raised there, I shall shift emphasis from the logic of comparative inquiry to the strategy of comparative inquiry.

I may begin by simply asserting a view of science, and the role methodology plays in it, that forms the basis of the analytic distinction employed in the discussion: the distinction between the logic

The first part of this chapter is adapted from Roger Benjamin, "Strategy versus Methodology in Comparative Research," *Comparative Political Studies* 9, no. 4 (January 1977): 475-84, by permission of the publisher, Sage Publications, Inc.

and strategy of inquiry. Recent work (Lakatos 1970; Moon 1975; and Ball 1976) suggests a way to reconcile the opposing relativistic (Kuhn 1970*a*, 1970*b*) and nomothetic/positivistic (Popper 1970) positions on the nature of scientific theory. The dilemma is that if one takes the view that scientific-theory change (i.e., paradigm shifts, acceptance or rejection of explanations, and the evaluation of theories) occurs primarily as a function of social system (Storer 1966), pragmatic (Mischel 1966), and hence nonrational forces, where does that leave the formal set of criteria—reconstructed logic known as the logic of inquiry? In fact, what is left that is distinctive about science? And where does that leave us in comparative research? An answer may rest with a Lakatosian response. The more "traditional" positivistic view of falsification, explanation, and the logic of inquiry is unpersuasive when taken alone, but if we adopt Lakatos's concept of scientific theory as comprising research programs that, having been granted their initial assumptions, can be subjected to scientific evaluation, logic of inquiry procedures can be brought to bear. Moreover, though the Kuhnian relativism position remains intact, concerning the nonrational criteria used to develop, test, and evaluate a theory (research program), we may evaluate research programs comparatively in terms of whether they are "progressive" or "degenerative" and whether they produce new and unintended "facts."

Especially in the absence of strong research programs, most "methods" work tends to consist of more or less elegant pleas for one research strategy or another. This is the case in comparative research, and thus I would place virtually all methodological discussion under the heading of strategy of inquiry. I do not mean that these discussions are unimportant; indeed the debate over how research methods may be combined in order to attack which principal questions necessarily composes the major share of activity in a field in which a strong research program is lacking. Nomothetic theory may be the ideal of science, but few fields approach it; in evaluating work one must ask the strategic question as well—how does it improve the level of knowledge in that particular field, given the particular inductive/deductive level of theory development the field has reached? I turn to review the criticisms of comparative methodology.

Limitations of the Comparative Method

Meckstroth suggests the limitations of comparative methodology for theory development in comparative research: the method

> provides no criteria to select among the limitless supply of attributes that might be introduced as controls or as explanations for any given phenomena. Thus all possibilities are equally relevant, as far as the method is concerned, and as long as an endless variety of possibilities must be considered, the method cannot justify conclusive statements about explanatory relationships. At best, therefore, the problem of identifying explanatory relationships is exacerbated, but is not created by a small number of cases, for the comparative method as previously defined does not provide sufficient conditions to discover these relationships under *any* circumstances. Instead, the method is completely dependent on criteria of relevance supplied by previously formulated concepts, propositions, and theories, which may be tested, but are not themselves discovered by the method alone. [1975, p. 134]

Teune, for his part, notes the extensive disagreements among those attempting to define comparative methodology and reformulates his own position concerning what comparative research should be about. "The direction of comparative research focused on establishing scientific generalizations should be toward system analysis of macro and micro process. . . cross-system (more than one country), cross-level (individual and the country or organization), and cross-time." Teune also restates the implications of nomothetic scientific-theory construction for comparative research, i.e., that it should attempt to make point predictions based on general theoretical statements (1975, pp. 197–98).

I accept Teune's statements as formulations of what comparative research should be about, and how to extend the canons of scientific inquiry to comparative research, but where does this take us? Are we left with any rationale for comparative methodology or, in fact, comparative research? If not, we are in difficulty, since comparative research is burgeoning.

Any remaining special claims of logical scientific relevance for comparative methodology would appear doubtful after Meckstroth also dealt persuasively with Lijphart's definitional claims for comparative methodology. Lijphart had stated "The comparative method is here defined as one of the basic methods—the others being the experimental, statistical and case study methods of establishing general propositions. Second, the comparative method is here defined as one of basic scientific methods and third, the comparative method is here regarded as establishing relationships among variables" (1971, p. 683). Lijphart (1975) acknowledges Meckstroth's criticism that these are assertions about the results of comparative methodology—not statements defining its logic.

The Strategy of Comparative Inquiry

Lijphart's (1975) response to Meckstroth (1975) fails to establish the case for a comparative methodology in the logic of inquiry sense but provides elements of a rationale in the strategy of inquiry sense. Lijphart begins by indicating what he believes comparative methodology is not. It is not coterminous with comparative politics, not even political science; not simply a perspective on a subject matter, a special set of substantive concerns, or a measurement system or statistical method; and not the case approach—though in its deviant-case form it remains a powerful tool of research. What the comparative method is, we are told, is the comparable-case method based on "selecting comparable cases for analysis and achieving a large measure of control as a result of their comparability." Therefore comparative methodology is "the method of testing hypothesized empirical relationships among variables on the basis of the same logic that guides the statistical method, but in which the causes are selected in such a way as to maximize the variance of the independent variables and to minimize the variance of the control variables" (pp. 163-64). To justify his argument, Lijphart criticizes use of the statistical method in comparative research, which he grants is superior to the comparable-case method because, whenever applicable, one can bring to bear the power of statistical inference. But this is where he fails to establish his point, not because his criticisms are invalid; in fact they are cogent. Rather, his criticisms must be regarded as strategic assessments of the way statistical methodology is employed, not as a critique of its logic. For example, Lijphart criticizes the whole-nation bias in comparative quantitative studies. To his point that these studies tend to be conducted at the nation-state level because of the availability of aggregate data—an illustration of tail-wagging in research, i.e., data availability determining the research problem selected—I would add only that comparative politics itself has long been overoriented toward the nation-state.[1]

The problem in Lijphart's criticism of statistical methodology is that he is really only pointing out the obvious difficulties of aggregate data analysis. Criticism of data analysis without consideration of the problem or the theory to which such analysis is attached is inappropriate. In the evaluation of any research there are reliability and validity issues, conceptual problems, or assumptional difficulties attached to the theoretical framework. What Lijphart is criticizing are the possible negative tradeoffs of one strategy of comparative research without fully examining the potential problems associated with his last candidate for comparative methodology, the comparable-case approach. He himself notes two difficulties: (1) the rarity of comparable-case settings and the possibility (probability?) that they will bias the selection of research problems; and (2) the *n*-problem, which he argues can be partially overcome by replication of the research in different settings.

In arguing the merits of the comparable-case method, Lijphart quotes Eulau approvingly to the effect that within-system comparisons, in settings like the American states, are ideal because they approach the comparable-case requirements closely. But one problem in within-system designs is concept equivalence. How can we be assured that the behavior encompassed under one conceptual term in system X captures the same behavior under the same conceptual term in system Y? As Goodenough (1970) points out with the example of cross-cultural marriage, we are not entitled to assume that this problem is easily resolvable. If statistical applications in comparative research err in forcing different behavior into standardized measurement categories, the comparable-case approach itself provides no criteria for ensuring that controlled settings can be matched elsewhere. The difficulty is that the more system-specific one becomes, to "minimize the variance of the control variables" (Lijphart 1975, p. 164), the more context-limited the applicability of the research design is likely to be. For example, the more one attempts to account for regional variation in political party institutionalization within Japanese prefectures, the greater one's tendency to work with endogenous conceptual categories that have meaning within the Japanese context but do not transfer easily to other systems.

Lijphart also suggests that the comparable-case approach will aid in solving the problem of overdetermination, identified by Przeworski and Teune (1970, p. 34) as follows: "Although the number of differences among similar countries is limited, it will almost invariably be sufficiently large to "overdetermine" the dependent phenomena. . . . There is more than one factor that ranks Great Britain, Australia, the United States, and Canada in the same order; there is more than one difference between the United States, Great Britain, and West Germany on the one hand, and Italy and Mexico on the other." Lijphart is not the first to advocate the use of subnational units of analysis, but what advantage does this strategy buy? Subnational units may be larger than many national units. Data problems may be as severe here as at the national level—for similar and different reasons. Moreover, one of the important issues in aggregate data analysis at the subnational level concerns the rules of aggregation and disaggregation to another level: the problem of cross-level inference (Teune 1975). A priori, I see no reason to believe that the ovedetermination problem will be solved by employment of subnational units.[2]

Finally, Lijphart's claims for logical status for the comparable-case method dissolve when one turns to the only basic rationale for comparative research in the first place: the process assumption elaborated below. This is also where the points Lijphart rejected for comparative methodology begin to make sense in considering the strategy of comparative research.

The Justification of Comparative Research

Let us assume that the claims for comparative methodology as a special case are unwarranted. If this is so, we must justify comparative research on some other basis. (Of course, there is the possibility that practitioners of comparative research are in the position of the subjects of the emperor with no clothes.) What does unite comparativists is the assumption that there are processes of organized complexity that are variable across systems, across levels, and across time. One need not assume one uniform curve along which all societies (or parts thereof) move; rather, *comparativists make the assumption that comparative analysis presents more variation to check and extend within-system-based findings.* By implication, this means that comparativists assume that single within-system designs capture only one process-state among the many that exist along multiple continua among and within the many social systems that exist across systems, levels, and time.

Ironically, the process assumption presents us with a variant of the Manheim paradox, forming at once arguments for and against theorizing about comparative sociopolitical change. The point to be emphasized concerns the scientific status of generalizations in sociopolitical change theory. As soon as we create a model, a representation of any particular process-state, we must be aware of the fact that the model will very probably be static, not dynamic. It is a difficult problem, well expressed recently by McCaughrin: "For the social scientists, priority is given to the realization of 'theory'—an explanatory system that is reliable throughout space and time. Yet if the development of society transforms events like revolution, then the quest for explanations that endure across time becomes problematic" (1976, p. 637). However, we shall see that there is a defense for comparative research.

The claim for the process assumption itself rests on the shared view of comparativists that while, for example, one may question specific causal linkages (e.g., the chain relating economic growth, urbanization, organizational involvement, and the growth of political awareness to increases in political participation [Nie, Powell, and Prewitt 1969]), few would deny that there are linkages among and between variables that tap the process itself. Acceptance of the process assumption suggests why one should be cautious about admitting relationships established on the basis of within-system (single-country) studies—namely that, since we do not know how or why the variables in the process described relate to one another across time, levels, and systems, how are we to interpret the comparative statistical relationships now being generated in comparative research? When we learn, for instance, that the positive relationships between voter participation and socioeconomic development established in American studies are reversed elsewhere (Milbrath 1965; cf. Benjamin et al. 1972), how are we to interpret this? Assuming competent research design construction and execution, one must also assume that unknown exogenous variable effects are at work. If one accepts the premise that there are multiple processes of change, the term "process" itself suggests multivariate rather than univariate systems of variable relationships.

In sum, the assumption that there exist multiple and dynamic processes suggests that (*a*) there are changes from one process-state to the next; (*b*) these changes constitute an important subject for comparative theory construction; and (*c*) this theory may not rest on variable relationships that account for any specific process; hence (*d*) theories that make point predictions about the strength as well as the direction of relationships are needed.

In one sense, the implications of the process assumption underlying comparative research might suggest its abandonment. Without theory we would continue to find it difficult to maintain strong confidence in our cross-system-based findings (where cross-level and cross-time designs may be undertaken as well). However, the alternative—not to engage in comparative research—is even more daunting, because the only way to check and extend system-specific-based findings is to do comparative research.

If these points have merit, we shall continue to discuss "comparative methodology" for the reasons Lijphart (1975) rejects, because the strategy problems of a field of study are as important as the methodological ones. For example, acceptance or rejection of specific comparative research findings is a function of prior "tacit" agreements reached by practitioners regarding evidence standards, appropriateness of methodologies applied, and so forth. The problem is that strategy discussions are concerned with the way to develop theory, and this fact makes such debates contentious. If we knew how to build theory, there would be no problem. The strategy of comparative inquiry belongs to the context of discovery, not the context of justification, where falsification procedures via a number of methods or research programs may be developed.

Recently, science was characterized as "purposive empiricism";[3] the development of every field consists of a constant search for grids that provide better coordinates with which to map and remap part of the "real" world of interest. This can only be understood as an iterative process. In comparative research the classification efforts of the 1950s and early 1960s, exemplified by Almond's work (Almond and Powell 1966), have been followed by comparative quantitative analysis, which is perhaps long on data and short on theory (Holt and Richardson 1970). Currently a number of strategies are being followed. Przeworski and his colleagues (Przeworski and Sprague 1971; Przeworski 1975) have carried out exercises in the tradition of operationalism—studies that must be regarded as standards for concept formation and measurement in comparative research. Putnam (1973) has shown that values can be studied systematically. Also promising are the recent applications of the collective goods approach. Using analytics that political scientists have regarded as powerful but empirically somewhat questionable, several examples serve as guides for further work to join rational-choice models to survey or aggregate data (Hirschman 1970; Breton 1974; Orbell and Uno 1972). Past and present work provides a stock of experiences supporting and undercutting a variety of solutions to problems, out of which the next generation of studies is launched. However, it is the assumption that there are common processes of political change that unites comparativists, rather than a method or logic of inquiry. This may clear the way for a less sterile and more field-specific search for the particular combination of methodological applications that will advance the subject. But it is important to summarize the lessons to be learned from a review of the issues of method and technique related to the study of sociopolitical change. The theory strategy undertaken here follows from an assessment of this literature.

Strategy, Method, and Technique Problems in Sociopolitical Change Studies

Analysis of sociological as well as logical dimensions in the comparative study of sociopolitical change suggests that the two must be joined if we are to understand some of our current methodological problems. The current *product* of comparative studies of sociopolitical change are criticized for being (1) atheoretic (Holt and Richardson 1970); (2) not truly comparative, because the studies are generally cross-sectional and face concept-equivalence problems (Brunner and Liepelt 1972);[4] (3) based on invalid linear and unicausal models of change that stem from an inappropriate unit and level of analysis, namely the national unit rather than sub- or transnational units that might reflect the parameters of the change process more sensitively (Benjamin et al. 1972); and (4) based on data from which investigators commit either the ecological or the individualistic fallacy (Meckstroth 1974). Methodological and technical advances remain sterile without substantive application; to emphasize solely the rich substantive components of the comparative study of sociopolitical change is to lose the potentially powerful aid that the methodological and technical advances of recent years could provide students.

The subfield of political development, like comparative politics as a whole, has gone through several phases, and now in the late 1970s we know more about what not to do and how not to do it, and consequently at least what we might try next. It is nevertheless sobering to realize, with Holt and Turner (1975), how little empirically grounded knowledge about political change we have developed. Let us review the major points of agreement and disagreement.

Conceptions of political change based on linear assumptions about development are not simply grounded upon questionable images and assumptions; the conceptions are false. To Huntington (1968) goes the credit for pointing out the need to build reversibility or decay into the concepts. Any definition must allow for negative as well as linear or inverse relationships between the political and socioeconomic related variable included in the study. I think there is also increasing consensus that unicausal explanations of sociopolitical change are excessively simplistic. Stimulated by the massive output of studies in the various social sciences, theorists in several fields have presented "explanations" of the fundamental causes of the basic dimensions of sociopolitical change. However, the unicausal explanations offered (e.g., the value system, attitude change, social structure, social stratification, or economic development) do not encompass the variance explained by the remaining plausible sources of change. Indeed a major problem now is to develop successful theory strategies to handle complex multivariate relationships while admitting at the same time the multidimensionality of the determinants of the change process.

The question of the proper unit of analysis is also receiving increased attention. Characteristics of the sociology of knowledge perhaps explain the excessive concentration on the national unit. The field of comparative politics derives largely from history, philosophy, and law. The major requirement was and is treating the whole political unit. There were and are only a few specialists on even such major political units as the Soviet Union, China, and the African and Latin American countries. The tendency of these specialists has been to study everything of political relevance to "their" country. Thus it has been natural for comparative theorists to assume that they should create theories to account for change at the national level. The problem is that aggregation of political behavior at this level of analysis is often unsuitable for theory development. None of the general theories developed in the 1960s has generated empirically corroborated findings, and I do not believe any will. For one thing, we have evidence that aggregation of political behavior at the national level obscures local and regional variation. Political change occurs at variable rates, with different impacts throughout the society.[5] There may be one, two, three, or more sequences of modernization, industrialization, or postindustrialization occurring at the same time in a society. I do not intend this to be an argument for any specific subnational unit of analysis; the research question itself must determine that. I will argue below, however, that the effort to disaggregate down from the entire political unit to institutions, groups, and even individual value systems (through cultural explanations) has not been very productive and that we should consider as an alternative the methodological individualistic strategy based on the collective goods approach.

The specific difficulties we face in concept formation and theory development are related both to the unit of analysis (the nation-state) that we have insisted on stressing and to the assumptions used to direct the analysis. The theory-based efforts used to study the nation-state are largely heuristic in content. It is difficult to imagine how the broad functional categories of the Almond scheme could be translated into empirically testable propositions. Recently a body of cross-national propositions has been generated that relies for the most part on cross-sectional data bases (Gillespie and Nesvold 1970), and this work has been criticized for being atheoretic. Correlations do not substitute for explanations of the relationships discovered between political participation and urbanization, communism and economic development, or democracy and socioeconomic levels of development. Nor in fact do other techniques such as factor analysis or causal modeling provide a substitute for theory; theory-based hypotheses may be falsified by causal models but not developed by the models themselves. Of course, one of the difficulties of comparative (cross-national) research is that of grounding any framework empirically so that it is capable of being tested. Problems of concept formation are also overwhelming at the national level of analysis. One man's political participation becomes another's concept of domestic conflict; no one has difficulty with voting as a participatory act, but what about demonstrations, strikes, riots, etc.? A major part of the problem is that we have inadequately conceived the units of behavior with which we wish to deal. Many of the measures that are assumed to tap different dimensions of the change process are actually intercorrelated (Przeworski and Teune 1970); many of these concepts and their accompanying measures tap the same underlying dimension and hence, in the language of statistics, create multicollinearity problems. And there is abundant evidence that the existence of data often influences concept and measurement decisions. Although, for example, virtually everyone agrees that voting is merely one portion of political participation, most investigators use only voting measures when studying the concept.

However, it may be at the data collection and analysis stage that work most clearly violates the process-analysis assumption. Most comparative research has relied on cross-sectional data sets. There are several difficulties in this corpus. At the concept level, there is the problem of concept equivalence. We know that political-party identification differs from one society to the next (Shively 1972) in terms of the empirical behavior it identifies. Political participation also varies in style and content. In the field of comparative public policy studies, for example, it would be useful to compare government policies toward social welfare cross-nationally by using fiscal data. However, in many societies much of what passes under the concept of social welfare is in fact accounted for by private traditional kinship groups. Small government expenditure patterns may miss this fact entirely, and invalid comparisons may result. In addition to the problem of concept equivalence, there are severe measurement difficulties. Census definitions of urbanization, voter turnout, occupational classification, and literacy differ from one society to the next. Survey-research students face the equally daunting problem of cross-cultural linguistic equivalence of terms when they undertake analysis. To compound difficulties, the quality of data collected from aggregate census sources, and possibly survey research as well, are autocorrelated with the socioeconomic development level of the society itself. Certainly the quality of census data is related, in a linear fashion, to the bureaucratic development level of existing political institutions. Moreover, many survey-research studies, such as the Almond and Verba (1963) study of political culture, in which they sought to measure the importance of civic culture, risk being tautological. One's propensity to respond in a relatively objective way to an interview request or questionnaire is in a basic sense a function of prior socialization patterns that would lead one to view such requests as reasonable. This kind of socialization experience is itself correlated positively with one's level of socioeconomic development; the greater the interaction between individuals throughout the society, the greater the information feedback mechanisms required. The result is that Americans spend much of their lives filling out forms, while residents of the Peruvian countryside do not. Studies based on these kinds of data thus tend to have conclusions built into them in an unintentional way. Finally, comparative studies of sociopolitical change would be in difficulty even if all of the foregoing problems were solved because of the implications of the process assumption when applied to problems of technique, which I shall now examine.

In the absence of a theory, cross-sectional studies assume stability in the relationships being studied. They also assume that the impact of exogenous variables may be treated as randomly distributed. This assumption is rarely accurate because of the problem of inadequate conception. But even if we may assume that we have properly delimited the variable in our system, so that no exogenous variable problems exist, this stability is questionable. We know intuitively that social reality is complex and unstable. The precise interrelations of a set of social and political variables may account for a single process-state and yet be inaccurate in forecasting either the continued existence of that particular process-state or precisely how it will change (Brunner and Liepelt 1972). To accomplish a correct forecast, we would need to know the parameters of the process under study; we would need a theory. For example, many studies proceed by separating out a common set of variables—perhaps urbanization, level of agriculture, per capita income, and political participation measures—from a cross-sectional data set based on large numbers of nations. The author executes his research design and then groups the nation-state according to the relationship found in the analysis. However, each variable in the analysis, particularly in the environment of rapid social-economic change facing political elites in modernizing and postindustrial societies, is likely to be highly unstable in relation to the other variables. Again, this does not mean we cannot use cross-sectional analysis; if we have specified a priori the strength (high, medium, or low) and direction of the relationships between our independent and dependent variables, cross-sectional data can be used. We should be alert to the fact that cross-system variation of within-system-generated relationships may wrongly imply system effects (uncontrolled exogenous variables or a different system state) instead of threshold effects (unstable variables or different process-states), as in our voting-participation example. Moreover, cross-time variation of within-system relationships may just as incorrectly imply threshold effects instead of aggregative effects, i.e., net macro (national) effects of linear but differently sloped micro (local) processes.

Because of the absence of theory and the inadequately conceived nature of our subject, both cross-sectional and cross-time analysis should be pursued in comparative settings. In this way we can improve our understanding of key relationships. For instance, the relationship between voting participation and socioeconomic development has been of continuing concern to American and other comparative research specialists. In the United States, based on findings in the 1950s and early 1960s, a general linear relationship between the various measures of socioeconomic development and political participation was suggested (Milbrath 1965). However, in the latter part of the 1960s students of French, Japanese, Malaysian, and Korean politics began to demonstrate empirically that this same relationship was inverse for the comparative analysis of political participation. In addition, study of the problem would be strengthened by use of nonlinear graphic techniques that illustrate the threshold points and the nonlinear shifts that appear to occur in the relationship.

Implications

We are now in a position to use the lessons arrived at here to engage in theory development in comparative research. Let me stress that I am not suggesting a "solution" to the vexing problem of how to make inferences between macro (system-level) and micro (individual-level) data. What I do argue is that the time has come to use a set of analytics—collective goods—that relies on aggregative rather than disaggregative principles. For example, instead of resorting to political-system characteristics to explain individual political attitudes and values, I look for specific sanctions and incentives that produce the rationale for individual behavior as the source of institutional or system characteristics. This book presents numerous examples of this approach. At base, the issue is epistemological; either one buys the inductive-statistical theories so familiar to most social scientists, or one is willing to take a fresh look at the merit of theory efforts of the hypothetico-deductive variety. I take two points as fundamental to any attempt to move beyond the present level of knowledge. First, we must use the process assumption as the basis for modeling comparative sociopolitical change; this will include construction of "new" provisional poles of the continua under study. Second, we will profit from a shift from the inductive-statistical strategy of theory generation to a theory source that emphasizes deductively generated point predictions of political behavior, a strategy that may also avoid some of the pitfalls of conception, methodology, measurement, and data analysis in the work just reviewed.

Notes

Chapter 2

1. There are a large and confusing number of definitions of rationality (Tisdale 1975; Goodin 1976) used to connect individual choice to goods. Here I shall stipulate the definition which becomes the basic assumption for the rest of the work: when confronted with the necessity of choice, individuals will calculate the ratio of benefits over costs of alternative *A* against the benefits over costs of alternative *B*. Note the comparative quality of the choice calculation. It is important to state also what this definition leaves out. Some rational-choice definitions, especially in economics (see Friedman 1953), make the assumption that the individual has perfect information. The relaxation of the perfect-information constraint places this rationality definition close to Simon's satisficing man. We satisfice by looking for alternatives in such a way that we can generally find an acceptable one after only moderate search (Simon 1969, p. 65).

2. Most collective goods applications in political science have worked with American data. For a review of much of this literature, see Ostrom and Ostrom 1971. Interesting applications in political inquiry include Ruggie 1972; and Orbell and Uno 1972. An excellent exposition of the collective goods alternative as an approach for theory development in comparative politics is in Harsanyi 1969. I will use the term "collective goods" rather than "public" or "rational choice," "political economy," or "public goods" to characterize the approach taken in this study for several reasons besides the technical definition presented here. Although I am indeed attempting to unite dimensions of economics and politics, much current work labeled political economy does not depart from the methodological individualism assumption of rational choice, nor does it develop composition statements through aggregation rather than disaggregation rules. Work in public choice is largely, though not wholly, devoted to American political and economic phenomena, and the major figures of the school tend to write from particular ideological perspectives. Finally, I agree with Henry about the use of the term "collective" versus "public" goods: "I have used the less familiar term 'collective goods' to refer to the various goods provided by government for members of society, some of which do and some of which do not fall into the category 'public good' in the different senses proposed by Samuelson and others" (1970, p. 275).

3. These points note the basic negative conditions leading to information bias and diseconomies of scale. Johnson (1975) lists representative positive conditions that contribute to bureaucratic growth for its own sake. Growth of an organization enhances the power of its leaders. Growth is also a generally accepted measure of the

demonstration of managerial competence. Growth is popular with existing staff because it creates new opportunities for advancement; this leads at a minimum to the sacrosanctity of existing budgetary allocations *and* to the toleration of wide margins of inefficiency.

4. Vincent Ostrom has suggested another interesting point to me. Professionalizing a task or set of tasks results in increased cost of the performance of activities because members of the newly created profession will find it in their interest to band together to raise their wages, limit further entry into their profession, and, as far as possible, protect their group from the vicissitudes of the market.

Chapter 3

1. Tipps 1973. Moreover, there are real-world limits to the applicability of this model. For example, diffusion models may be more appropriate for understanding the developing pattern of smaller industrial states in western Europe and elsewhere. In these highly penetrated societies, mass publics and elites will presumably react to already established models of society and politics. Dependency relationships between states will also alter the future pattern of sociopolitical change of many societies.

2. Kumar, in an excellent cautionary article (1976), disputes the view that there has been the threshold change that I am arguing. He cites evidence, for example, that the service sector has been growing since the beginning of the Industrial Revolution in societies such as Britain. However, it is the emergence of the service sector as the central force in the economy that is the most important change. Kumar himself notes the late changing values—in the subconscious, as he puts it—toward the postindustrial value syndrome described above. However, as I argue in chap. 5, the values of individuals do not change unless there are incentives and/or sanctions which compel them to do so; in short, structural change promotes changes in values, and not vice versa. Kumar (1978) has gone on to develop an excellent overview of the sociological dimensions of industrial and postindustrial society. His work, which came to my attention after I finished this study, is a useful complement to the points made here.

3. Sproule-Jones summarizes the case for polycentricity in the design of political institutions: "Legal authority is fragmented among federal, state, and in many cases, local sets of institutions, themselves fragmented into executive, legislative and judicial departments. None of these enjoys independence in the making of particular decisions. An individual who finds a decision made in one center unacceptable to his interests has the constitutional capacity to take his case to an alternative forum. The combined effect of these multiple decision structures, all of which are potent but nonomnipotent centers of power, is to require the support for any public policy or choice of more than a mere majority of interested citizens. Any disaffected party to an economic transaction can exercise a veto-like position for he can wield a potential threat of involving the other parties in protracted and risky political ventures. These potential political costs create a substantial incentive, therefore, to come to terms with their public or clientele, and with agencies and public officials jointly serving the clientele. Even though behavior of the public enterprises may, as a consequence, appear imperialistic, such behavior need not, in short, be seen as pathological, but as a type of public analogue of private competitive entrepreneurial behavior" (1972, pp. 185–86).

4. There is much formal work to be done on both the question of the optimum size

of the government unit for distributing different types of goods and the analysis of criteria for economies and diseconomies of scale. The theory of the firm provides an opportunity for attacking the latter issue, and the theory of clubs is suggestive for examining the size problem of government units. E.g., Buchanan (1965) suggests an inverse relationship between the degree of societal affluence and the size of club membership preferred by individual members of groups.

Chapter 4

1. Rao's technique assumes a sample of units used to calculate the correlation which defines the space in which the factors are to be placed. Because of missing-data problems, a pairwise deletion technique was used, so that where an observation on a single variable is missing for any country, the country is removed only from calculations of the correlation coefficients on that variable. This factor is based on the assumption that the variance of each variable has associated common, unique, and error variance. The multiple R^2 is used to estimate the reliable common variance of all other variables on each variable prior to the factor analysis (Rummel 1970). By the Kaiser criterion, only those factors with eigenvalues above unity were rotated to final solution. Rao's canonical factor method allows for the testing of the statistical significance, and the two factors extracted and rotated proved significance at higher than the .005 level. A common criticism of factor analysis concerns the assumptions of linearity and the interval nature of the data. Since I am using this technique to group and rank the countries in the data set (table 3), I corroborated the factor analysis with small-space analysis, a multidimensional scaling technique which is based on nonmetric assumptions. (The results, not reproduced here, corroborate the factor analysis results.) Only ranking need be presented in transforming proximates to distances. The distances are calculated in a specified dimensionality, and when undimensionality is not assumed, a metric must be selected in order to measure interpoint distances in *n*-dimensional space. This procedure actually raises the level of measurement; the distances so computed are interval-level measures "recovered" from the ordinal measures actually added originally (see Young 1963). Here I am interested in the possible effects of single factors on a single dependent or criterion variable. If there are no differences between the populations being compared—in this case postindustrialization, industrialization, modernization—the bias terms will be zero. If *FE* (the *F* test) is larger than 1, we may reason that the variation among the population means is large. For the definition of the critical value which I used to decide whether F_0 is significantly larger than 1, see Yamane 1973, p. 836. The data are from Taylor and Hudson 1972.

Chapter 5

1. One might also use a game-theoretic approach here, but it would appear most appropriate when the real-world setting approximating zero or nonzero sum conditions is already specified. Collective goods distinctions prove more powerful in deducing the change that occurs in cognitive orientations in their development over time. E.g., consider this quote from Wilson and Banfield (1964), who argue that we need to "know more about each of the various *subcultures* [emphasis added], especially about the nature of the individual's attachments to the society, his concept of what is

just, and the extent of the obligation he feels to subordinate his interests to that of various others (e.g., the community)." Cf. Silverman (1968), who observes the same amoral behavior as Banfield (1958); e.g., individuals maximize the material, short-run advantages of the nuclear family, and village social systems appear lacking in moral sanctions outside the immediate family; but Silverman argues that this "ethos" is a function of their system of agricultural organization and that changes in social patterns and values will follow from agricultural reorganization. Silverman shifts attention to institutions, to the way a collective action unit is organized. This emphasis goes part way to the position taken by Harsanyi, which I adopt here: "Explaining social institutions essentially amounts to explaining changes in these institutions and these changes themselves must be ultimately explained in terms of personal incentives for some people to change their behavior" (1969, p. 532). We also have supporting evidence from social psychology suggesting that when the urban poor are placed in an adequate goods environment, they operate with a delayed-gratification pattern or future orientation equivalent to their middle-class counterparts. In fact, given any semblance of a secure resource base, the urban poor appear to engage in more deferred-gratification behavior than the middle class, who can afford the short-term consumption pattern they often engage in because of the slack provided by a larger resource base. "The situational variable. . .determines the ability to delay" (Miller, Riessman, and Seagull 1965, p. 300; cf. the literature reviewed in Irelan 1967). Yet another perspective that might be used to examine the problem discussed in this chapter is that of property-rights theory. Developed by some of the same theorists active in more general collective goods theory and congruent with the analysis presented here, this theory emphasizes the importance of property systems in determining the distribution of authority and power within societies. Perhaps especially in rural and largely traditional societies—like the one dealt with by Foster (1965)—property is defined broadly to include all those things, e.g., object, resources, and events to which individuals may have legal claim and which traditional authority (government) supports. However, the lessons of property rights theory are more applicable to the world of the adequate good where property is divided up among citizens. For an application, see Loveman 1976, pp. 3–21. For a review and critique of property-rights theory, see Furniss 1978.

2. I shall not discuss two logical possibilities afforded by an environment that presents such a high degree of scarcity as to preclude any organizational attempts to cope, or the improbable case of the society that confronts no scarcity at all. Nor will I discuss the conditions under which those holding the adequate-good image may move to the limited-good image.

3. E.g., Waterbury (1975) develops a comparative description that corroborates the foregoing points: Oaxaca peasants remained nonrevolutionary under the image of limited good, as compared with inhabitants of Morelos, because the negative institutional changes in the environment facing the Morelos peasants forced them to act.

4. By placing this intragroup violence under the limited-good image, I agree with recent revisions that argue that one must regard deviant behavior in terms of class categories, and hence as political. See Taylor and Taylor 1973. However, I agree with Harsanyi (1969) that class concepts are crude surrogates for collective action models. Class analysis does in fact begin with the assumption of individual rationality.

5. Hobsbawn puts it another way: "Becoming a revolutionary implies not only a

measure of despair, but also some hope. The typical alternation of passivity and activism among some notoriously oppressed classes is thus explained" (1973, p. 248). Of course the American urban poor may be worse off economically than the middle class and yet relatively better off than the middle class in Third World countries, which suggests that we must reintroduce the concept of relative inequality in urban settings.

6. It should be emphasized that this model does not encompass all urban violence. Some violence is directed at members of the same race who are viewed as exploiters; there is also violence directed against symbols of external authority. These types of violence are not mutually exclusive, as indicated in fig. 8.

Chapter 6

1. Definitional exercises unattached to theoretical meaning can be sterile and devoid of content. However, such exercises are useful if they fulfill at least three conditions. First, it is useful to reexamine assumptions underlying basic concepts that structure subfields of inquiry in the light of new approaches or theories that might illuminate the concept. Second, reworking the concept in conjunction with the theory may help to reorganize our understanding of existing work based on the concept. Third, a reconceptualization that points the way toward new hypotheses and measurement and data-collection procedures would also be helpful. Moreover, it is important to extend our thinking about the "developmental" implications of new "poles" in the sociopolitical change process even if the model constructed is not descriptive of the choices facing most citizens in societies not in the postindustrial phase. Especially in the interdependent world in which we live, different "developmental" issues such as those charted below become symbolic images to which elites in all societies react.

2. The literature on the concept of development is of course large. In addition to the work of Apter (1965, 1974), Huntington's (1968, 1971) and Kesselman's (1973) remain among the most important statements on the subject by political scientists. Tipps's (1973) essay summarizes the thinking in the other fields of social science. Inkeles and Wilbert Moore provide representative examples of models of individual change that may be accurate descriptions of the modernization and industrialization process-states of sociopolitical change, but they are not very useful for the postindustrial process-state. Inkeles notes the following as definitional qualities of modern man: "readiness for new experience and openness to innovation and change" (1976, p. 327); more orientation to the present and future—accepting fixed hours and schedules, being "punctual, regular, and orderly in organizing his affairs" (p. 329); ability to plan and "learn to dominate his environment in order to advance his own purpose and goals" (ibid.). Moore, for his part, lists among the more "specific values and principles of conduct appropriate to modernization, . . . rationalization in problem solving, punctuality, recognition of individuality limited by systematically linked interdependence, and achievement and mobility aspirations" (quoted by Inkeles, p. 335). However, beyond "modernization," do we not need a model of man's problems of choice? Is there not a point at which additional interdependence becomes a loss rather than a gain? How much punctuality is enough? What happens after man learns to dominate his environment? At what point does additional information

become costly for the individual to code and store, i.e., a problem itself rather than a positive benefit? All these questions suggest the need for a new provisional benchmark for individual change beyond modernity.

3. See Maslow 1954. Barrington Moore, Jr. touches on this theme in the quotation on p. 51: "At the level of straightforward biological needs, such as those of sleep, food, and sex, there is an obvious upper limit of satiation. More subtle and cultural and psychological needs, such as those for affection and admiration, do not have such clear upper limits. *On the other hand, these vary with changing historical conditions*" (B. Moore 1965, p. 185; emphasis added). The point to emphasize is the effect of environment on the nature of individual wants.

4. I have adapted the concept of access from Williams (1971), who has used it in an imaginative fashion to reconceive our thinking about urban politics.

5. The economist's treatment of much service as "nonprogressive," i.e., nonincreasing in productivity, is erroneous. If services are contributing to individual efforts to procure wants that are no longer directed mainly at increasing the consumption of material goods, perhaps we should begin to think about the basis for our productivity-measurement criteria. Now it remains heavily biased in favor of areas of the economy that, through increasing economies of scale, achieve increases in productivity across time (Fuchs 1968).

6. "The principal opposition between these two great classes (managers and workers)...does not result from the fact that one possesses wealth or property and the other does not. It comes about because the *dominant classes dispose of knowledge and control information*" (Touraine 1974, p. 61). One might also object that the amount and complexity of information under an individual's control is autocorrelated with the level of education achieved. However, another hallmark of postindustrialization is the uniformly high level of formal education achieved—up to and including postgraduate work. I would add that much work remains to be done to operationalize the information variable.

7. E.g., a recent University of Minnesota dissertation found that the average time spent going to and from work has remained roughly *constant* in the Los Angeles area from 1870 to 1970, while the distance traveled has expanded enormously: see Dale 1971.

Chapter 7

1. Early work on interest groups in this century precedes excellent statements in the post-World War II period: see Bently 1908; followed by Herring 1929; Truman 1951; and Latham 1952. Dahl 1961 and Polsby 1963 present the strongest defense of pluralism itself.

2. It is also the point at which the other images or metaphors of the organization of the economy and polity that stress centralization are appropriate. See Galbraith 1967; and Huntington 1968.

Chapter 8

1. Note, further, the following associated conclusion: "In services where size of population is especially important, once an authority's population goes much above 1,000,000 further gains in functional efficiency are unlikely to offset disadvantages associated with the management of such large units.... The concentration of work in

a single authority in charge of all local government services could be too great if the authority was responsible for both an extensive area and for a population of well over a million. It could have serious managerial problems due to the sheer size and complexity of the organization it would have to maintain. Perhaps they could be overcome but much continuing effort would have to go into solving them." Why are these problems considered relevant for bureaucratic organizations serving areas with populations in excess of 1 million? Why not 500,000, or even less, or, for that matter, what grounds did the commission have for saying there would be any additional problems in a population area of more than 1 million?

2. To my knowledge the concept of efficiency is nowhere defined by those writing about English local government. It is a difficult problem; is the police force that arrests more individuals more successful than the one that arrests fewer, perhaps as a result of crime-prevention methods? One way to view the concept is in terms of the organization's *success* in making choices that yield a higher proportion of benefits over cost vis-à-vis its stated organizational goals.

3. It is important to note two additional points that Vincent Ostrom called to my attention. First, absolute social and economic equality is probably not only impossible but also undesirable, for reasons that I shall not list here, because of the length needed to cover such a topic. Second, postindustrialization may actually increase the number of poor in all remaining unorganized groups in society, e.g., the young, the aged, women, and minorities.

4. Ostrom 1972. For some Ostrom's polycentricity offers an apologia for the fragmented world of American local government. In fact it is the start of needed design work to develop a new structuring principle from which local government reform may proceed (Self 1975).

Chapter 9

1. The term "service" itself is more misleading than the concepts "agricultural" and "industrial." From its first usage (see Hartwell 1971; and Kumar 1976) the service concept has been the residual category into which disparate elements have been dumped. E.g., research and development produces technically progressive economic activity, while Kumar (1976) notes that many things listed under research and development are really only marketing activities.

2. However, I have also argued the importance of the growth of interdependence, which suggests that it is becoming increasingly difficult to determine what is not a crucial economic function. In the end, New Yorkers would really be hard put to choose between doing without electricity and doing without garbage collection.

3. Renewed attention to the tradeoffs between equality and liberty is surfacing: see Rawls 1971; and Nozick 1974.

4. I am well aware of the frequent fate of optimists and seers, and yet the need for visions of future states is crucial in times of such rapid sociopolitical change. Such visions in social science may be considered analogous to architectural blueprints; they are anticipatory and are built on the best estimates gleaned from analysis of emergent properties perceived in the present.

5. Surprisingly, studies of social-economic change and deviance have remained separate. Surely it is not unreasonable to expect a close correlation between the rate and sequence of social-economic change and the disruptive change produced. The

greater the pace of change, the greater the level of "pathologies" such as family breakdown, crime, alcoholism, and mental illness. Though I do not know of any specific research that tests this assertion, underlying much of the deviance (sometimes called social control) literature is the assumption that the pace of change has a good deal to do with society's problems.

6. Galbraith 1967. Much of this work focuses on the political institutional design implications of postindustrialization. I do not mean to suggest that the political power concentrated in corporations in the private sector is not an important issue; it is important and will remain so. However, here I wish to draw attention to the very significant design questions confronting the public sector. Moreover, I believe that the political problems discussed here will be more important than the market issues elucidated by Lindblom (1977).

7. Frolich, Oppenheimer, and Young 1971. Here I borrow from Herbert Simon and C. West Churchman, who have thought about what the design of artificial systems means. For them design and nature are not antithetical. Design is "allied to conscious." What aspect of an inquiring system cannot be made conscious? This is the "natural" question about design. Hence design too is a natural function for us all (Churchman 1971, p. 276). The world of politics is itself artifactual, and thus I take institutional and leadership design questions to be "natural" in Churchman's sense. Cf. Simon 1969.

Postscript

1. O'Connor (1973) called attention to the problem. Generally, the societies referred to in this discussion include Britain, Germany, France, Sweden, Denmark, and North America (excluding Mexico), plus Japan. For economy of presentation, I shall refer mainly to work done by American and British scholars.

2. See esp. Huntington 1975; Bell 1975; King 1975; Rose and Peters 1978; and Winkler 1977. Irving Kristol, Daniel Moynihan, and James Q. Wilson often write in *Public Interest.*

Appendix

1. Lijphart points out that regional variation can be obscured by collapsing subnational data in nation-unit averages.

2. I do not mean to suggest that subnational studies are not valuable. Indeed there has been an overemphasis on nation-state units of analysis.

3. Maxwell 1974. The specific strategy of inquiry used here exemplifies this point concerning the relationship of theory and sociopolitical change. Although I argue that our greatest need is to estimate process-states from theory, not data, I actually develop the postindustrial model from empirical evidence and hence inductive reasoning. I then interpret the political impact of postindustrialization through collective goods analytics, a deductive theory strategy. However, this description of an iterative reasoning process really captures the way anyone concerned with comparative theory development operates.

4. The direction in which the position of Brunner and Liepelt leads us is highlighted by comparing the views of an important comparative politics theorist with the stand of an influential economist on the relevance of statistically based explanation.

In addition to reiterating that the political system is the emerging analytical framework, Almond argues that the statistical approach will be the dominant mode of explanation in political research; he also points to agreement concerning the need to engage in "the differentiation and specification of variables and the assumptions of probability and reflexivity in their relations" (Almond 1966, p. 876). Compare, however, the following view of statistical explanation. "Statistics, however, deals with the problem of large numbers essentially by eliminating complexity and deliberately treating the individual elements which it counts as if they were not systematically connected. It avoids the problem of complexity by substituting for the information on the individual elements information on the frequency with which their different properties occur in classes of such elements, and it deliberately disregards the fact that the *relative* position of the different elements in a structure may matter" (Hayek 1967, p. 29; emphasis added). Hayek would, I believe, side with Brunner and Liepelt against Almond. Differentiation and specification of variables may be well and good, but unless one has a priori assumptions about the *particular* level of probability between variables, one violates the lessons of the process assumption; there is no substitute for theory strategies of the hypothetico-deductive variety. Hayek also notes the areas where statistics can assist us, e.g., "where we had information about many complex structures of the same kind" and "where the complex phenomena and not the elements of which they consist could be made the elements of the statistical collective." But, he adds, this "presupposes that we have an independent criterion for identifying structures of the kind in question" (p. 30). The misconception of the use of statistics comes when we think of social and political systems. "Nobody would probably seriously contend that statistics can elucidate even the comparatively not very complex structures of organic molecules"; however, "when it comes to accounting for the functioning of social structures, the belief is widely held" (ibid., p. 31).

5. Moreover, we should also abandon our preoccupation with within-system variation and the national-boundary assumption. There are no political units unaffected by penetration by the international system. This is not only true in Third World countries, where economic, social, and political institutions appear to be challenged for different reasons, but in industrial and postindustrial societies as well. Only in the past few years has attention been given to the impact of foreign aid, human-resource transfers, and multinational corporations on various elements of the political change process both within and across (cross-national) systems.

Bibliography

Almond, Gabriel A. 1966. "Political Theory and Political Science." *American Political Science Review* 60 (December): 873–78.

Almond, Gabriel A., and Powell, G. Bingham, Jr. 1966. *Compara-Tive Politics: A Developmental Approach.* Boston: Little, Brown & Co.

Almond, Gabriel [A.], and Verba, Sidney. 1963. *The Civic Culture.* Princeton: Princeton University Press.

Anderson, Charles N. 1977. "Political Design and the Representation of Interests." *Comparative Political Studies* 10 (April): 127–52.

Apter, David P. 1965. *The Politics of Modernization.* Chicago: University of Chicago Press.

———. 1971. *Choice and the Politics of Allocation.* New Haven: Yale University Press.

Armstrong, Scott J. 1967. "Derivation of Theory by Means of Factor Analysis, or Tom Swift and His Electric Factor Analysis Machine." *American Statistician* (December), pp. 17–21.

Arrow, Kenneth J. 1951. *Social Choice and Individual Values.* New Haven: Yale University Press.

Ashford, D. A. 1975. "Parties and Participation in British Local Government and Some American Parallels." *Urban Affairs Quarterly* 11:58–81.

Bains Committee. 1972. *The New Local Authorities: Management and Structure.* London: Her Majesty's Stationery Office.

Ball, Terrence. 1976. "From Paradigms to Research Programs: Toward a Post-Kuhnian Political Science." *American Journal of Political Science* 20 (February): 151–77.

Banfield, Edward C. 1958. *The Moral Basis of a Backward Society.* Glencoe, Ill.: Free Press.

———. 1960. "The Management of Metropolitan Conflict." *Daedalus* 90 (Winter): 61–78.

———. 1970. *The Unheavenly City: The Nature and Future of Our Urban Crisis.* Boston: Little, Brown & Co.

Baumol, William J. 1967. "Macroeconomics of Unbalanced Growth: The Anatomy of Urban Crisis." *American Economic Review* 57 (June): 415-26.

———. 1969. *Welfare Economics and the Theory of the State.* Cambridge, Mass.: Harvard University Press.

Beer, Samuel H. 1969. *British Politics in the Collective Age.* New York: Alfred A. Knopf.

Bell, Daniel. 1973. *The Coming of Post-industrial Society.* New York: Basic Books.

———. 1975. "The Revolution of Rising Entitlements." *Fortune* (April), p. 98.

Benjamin, Roger. 1975. "The Political Consequences of Postindustrialization." *International Review of Community Development* 33-34 (Winter): 149-58.

———. 1976. "Cognitive Orientations and the Impact of Scarcity on Politics." *Social Science Quarterly* 57 (September): 397-409.

———. 1977*a*. *Government and Collective Goods in Postindustrial Society.* Occasional Paper 15. Pittsburgh: International Studies Association, University Studies Association, University of Pittsburgh.

———. 1977*b*. "Local Government in Postindustrial Britain: Studies of the British Royal Commission on Local Government." Pp. 149-72 in *Comparing Urban Service Delivery Systems,* ed. Vincent Ostrom and Frances Bish. Urban Affairs Annual Reviews, vol. 12. Beverly Hills, Calif.: Sage Publications, Inc.

———. 1977*c*. "Strategy versus Methodology in Comparative Research." *Comparative Political Studies* 9 (January): 475-84.

Benjamin, Roger, et al. 1972. *Patterns of Political Development.* New York: David McKay.

Bently, Arthur F. 1908. *The Process of Government.* Chicago: University of Chicago Press.

Boulding, Kenneth. 1956. *The Image.* Ann Arbor: University of Michigan Press.

Breton, Albert. 1974. *The Economic Theory of Representative Government.* Chicago: Aldine Publishing Co.

Brewer, Garry D., and Brunner, Ronald. 1976. *Political Development and Change: A Political Approach.* New York: Free Press.

Brittan, Samuel. 1975. "The Economic Contradictions of Democracy." *British Journal of Political Science* 5 (April): 129-59.

———. 1977. *The Delusion of Incomes Policy.* Oxford: Oxford University Press.

Brunner, Ronald D., and Liepelt, Klaus. 1972. "Data Analysis, Process Analysis, and System Change." *Midwest Journal of Po-*

litical Science 16 (November): 538–69.

Brzezinski, Zbigniew. 1970. *Between Two Ages: America's Role in the Technetronic Era.* New York: Viking Press.

Buchanan, James M. "An Economic Theory of Clubs." 1965. *Economica* 32 (February): 1–15.

Caporaso, James, and Duvall, Raymond. 1972. "Time and Social Change." Unpublished manuscript, Department of Political Science, University of Minnesota.

Churchman, C. West. 1971. *The Design of Inquiring Systems.* New York: Basic Books.

Cloward, Richard A., and Piven, Frances F. 1974. *The Politics of Turmoil.* New York: Pantheon Books.

Coleman, James. 1972. "Collective Decisions and Collective Action." Pp. 208–19 in *Philosophy, Politics and Society,* ed. Peter Laslett, William G. Runciman, and Quentin Skinner. Oxford: Basil Blackwell.

Coulter, Phillip. 1972. "Political Development and Political Theory: Methodological and Technological Problems in the Comparative Study of Political Development." *Polity* 5 (Winter): 233–49.

Current Anthropology. 1969. Vol. 10 (April–June).

Dahl, Robert A. 1961. *Who Governs?* New Haven: Yale University Press.

Dahrendorf, Rolf. 1975. *The New Liberty: Survival and Justice in a Changing World.* Stanford, Calif.: Stanford University Press.

Dale, James E. 1971. "Space Ship Earth or Mother Earth: An Analysis of the Ecological Problem." Ph.D. dissertation, University of Minnesota.

Deutsch, Karl. 1963. *The Nerves of Government.* New York: Free Press.

Downs, Anthony. 1967. *Inside Bureaucracy.* Boston: Little, Brown & Co.

———. 1969. "The Coming Revolution in City Planning." Pp. 596–610 in *Urban Governments,* ed. Edward C. Banfield. New York: Free Press.

Dunn, William. 1976. "The Future Which Began: Notes on Development Policy and Social Systems Delimitation." Paper presented at the National Conference of the American Society for Public Administration, April, Washington, D.C.

Eckstein, Harry. 1960. *Pressure Group Politics: The Case of the British Medical Association.* London: George Allen & Unwin.

Etzioni, Amitai. 1977–78. "Societal Overload." *Political Science Quarterly* 92 (Winter): 607–33.

Foster, George M. 1965. "Peasant Society and the Image of Limited

Good." *American Anthropologist* 67 (April): 293–315.

———. 1972. "A Second Look at Limited Good." *Anthropological Quarterly* 45 (April): 57–64.

Friedman, Milton M. 1953. *Essays in Positive Economics.* Chicago: University of Chicago Press.

Frolich, Norman; Oppenheimer, Joseph; and Young, Oran. 1971. *Political Leadership and Collective Goods.* Princeton: Princeton University Press.

Fuchs, Victor R. 1968. *The Service Economy.* New York: National Bureau of Economic Research.

Furniss, Norman. 1978. "The Political Implications of the Public Choice–Property Rights School." *American Political Science Review* 72 (June): 399–410.

Galbraith, John K. 1967. *The New Industrial State.* Boston: Houghton Mifflin Co.

Gillespie, John, and Nesvold, Betty, eds. 1970. *Comparative Macro Quantitative Analysis.* Beverley Hills, Calif.: Sage Publications.

Goodenough, Ward H. 1970. *Description and Comparison in Cultural Anthropology.* Chicago: Aldine Publishing Co.

Goodin, Richard E. 1976. *The Politics of Rational Man.* New York: John Wiley & Sons.

Great Britain. Central Statistical Office. 1975. *Annual Abstract of Statistics.* London: Her Majesty's Stationery Office.

Gupta, S. P., and Hutton, J. P. 1968. *Economics of Scale in Local Government Services.* Research Study 3, Institute of Social and Economic Research, University of York. London: Her Majesty's Stationery Office.

Gurr, Ted R. 1970. *Why Men Rebel.* Princeton: Princeton University Press.

Habermas, Jürgen. 1970. *Toward a Rational Society: Student Protest, Science, and Politics.* Boston: Beacon Press.

———. 1975. *Legitimation Crisis.* Boston: Beacon Press.

Halmos, Paul. 1966. *The Personal Service Society.* Inaugural lecture delivered at University College. Cardiff: University of Wales Press.

Hancock, M. Donald, and Sjoberg, Gordon, eds. 1972. *Politics in the Post-Welfare State.* New York: Columbia University Press.

Hardin, Grant. 1968. "The Tragedy of the Commons." *Science* 162 (December 13): 1243–48.

Harrington, Michael. 1976. *The Twilight of Capitalism.* New York: Simon & Schuster.

Harsanyi, John C. 1969. "Rational-Choice Models of Political Behavior vs. Functionalist and Conformist Theories." *World Poli-*

tics 21 (July): 91–108.

Hartwell, Ronald Maxwell. 1971. *The Industrial Revolution and Economic Growth.* London: Methuen Co.

Hayek, F. A. *The Road to Serfdom.* 1944. London: Routledge & Kegan Paul.

———. 1967. *Studies in Philosophy, Politics, and Economics.* Chicago: University of Chicago Press.

Heath, Anthony. 1976. *Rational Choice and Social Exchange: A Critique of Exchange Theory.* Cambridge: Cambridge University Press.

Heilbroner, Robert L. 1977. "The False Promise of Growth." *New York Review of Books* (March 3), p. 10.

Henry, Nannerl O. 1970. "Political Obligation and Collective Goods." Pp. 272–87 in *Political and Legal Obligation,* ed. J. Roland Pennock and John W. Chapman. New York: Atherton Press.

Herring, E. Pendleton. 1929. *Group Representation before Congress.* Baltimore: Johns Hopkins Press.

Hibbs, Douglas. 1976. "Industrial Conflict in Advanced Industrial Societies." *American Political Science Review* 70 (December): 1033–58.

Hill, Dolores M. 1973. *Participating in Local Affairs.* London: Penguin Books.

Hill, Richard C. 1974. "Separate and Unequal: Governmental Inequality in the Metropolis." *American Political Science Review* 68 (December): 1557–68.

Hirsch, Fred. 1976. *Social Limits to Growth.* Cambridge, Mass.: Harvard University Press.

Hirschman, Albert O. 1970. *Exit, Voice and Loyalty.* Cambridge, Mass.: Harvard University Press.

Hirschman, Albert O., and Rothschild, Michael. 1973. "The Changing Tolerance for Economic Inequality in the Course of Economic Development." *Quarterly Journal of Economics* 87 (November): 544–66.

Hobsbawn, E. H. 1973. *Revolutionaries.* New York: New American Library.

Holmes, Paul. 1966. *The Personal Service Society.* Inaugural lecture delivered at University College. Cardiff: University of Wales Press.

Holt, Robert T., and Richardson, John E. 1970. "Competing Paradigms in Comparative Politics." Pp. 22–72 in *The Methodology of Comparative Research,* ed. Robert T. Holt and John E. Turner. New York: Free Press.

Holt, Robert T., and Turner, John E. 1975. "Crises and Sequences in Collective Theory Development." *American Political Science Review* 69 (September): 979-94.

Huntington, Samuel P. 1968. *Political Order in Changing Societies.* New Haven: Yale University Press.

———. 1971. "The Change to Change: Modernization, Development, and Politics." *Comparative Politics* 3 (April): 283-322.

———. 1974. "Postindustrial Politics: How Benign Will It Be?" *Comparative Politics* 6 (January): 163-91.

———. 1975. "The Democratic Distemper." *Public Interest* 14 (Fall): 9-38.

Ike, Nobutake. 1973. "Economic Growth and Intergenerational Change in Japan." *American Political Science Review* 67 (December): 1194-1203.

Inglehart, Ronald. 1971. "The Silent Revolution in Europe: Intergenerational Change in Post-industrial Societies." *American Political Science Review* 65 (December): 991-1017.

———. 1977*a*. *The Silent Generation in Europe.* Princeton: Princeton University Press.

———. 1977*b*. "Values, Objective Needs, and Subjective Satisfaction among Western Publics." *Comparative Political Studies* 9 (January): 429-58.

Inkeles, Alex. 1976. "A Model of the Modern Man: Theoretical and Methodological Issues." Pp. 320-48 in *Comparative Modenization,* ed. C. E. Black. New York: Free Press.

Inkeles, Alex, and Smith, David H. 1974. *Becoming Modern.* Cambridge, Mass.: Harvard University Press.

Institute of Local Government Studies, University of Birmingham. 1968*a*. *Administration in a Large Local Authority: A Comparison with Other Country Boroughs.* Research Study 7. London: Her Majesty's Stationery Office.

———. 1968*b*. *Aspects of Administration in a Large Local Authority.* Research Study 7. London: Her Majesty's Stationery Office.

International Labour Office. 1972. *Yearbook of Labour Statistics.* Geneva: ILO.

Irelan, Lola M., ed. 1967. *Low-Income Life Styles.* Washington, D.C.: Department of Health, Education, and Welfare.

Israel, Joachim. 1974. "The Welfare State—a Manifestation of Late Capitalism." *ACTA Sociologica* 17, no. 4:310-29.

Johnson, Harry G. 1975. *On Economics and Society.* Chicago: University of Chicago Press.

Jones, G. W. 1973. "The Local Government Act of 1972 and the Redcliffe-Maud Commission." *Political Quarterly* 44 (April-

June): 154-66.

Kelley, Donald L.; Stunkel, Kenneth R.; and Wescott, Richard R. *The Economic Superpowers and the Environment.* San Francisco: W. H. Freeman 1976.

Kesselman, Mark. 1970. "Overinstitutionalization and Political Constraint: The Case of France." *Comparative Politics* 3 (October): 21-45.

———. 1973. "Order or Movement? The Literature of Political Development as Ideology." *World Politics* 26 (October): 139-54.

King, Anthony. 1975. "Overload: Problems of Governing in the 1970's." *Political Studies* 23 (June-September): 162-74.

Kohlberg, Laurence. 1969. "Stage and Sequence: The Cognitive Developmental Approach to Socialization." Pp. 347-480 in *Handbook of Socialization Theory and Research,* ed. David Goslin. New York: Rand McNally.

Kuhn, Thomas. 1970*a*. "Reflections on My Critics." Pp. 231-78 in *Criticism and the Growth of Knowledge,* ed. Imre Lakatos and Alan Musgrave. Cambridge: Cambridge University Press.

———. 1970*b*. *The Structure of Scientific Revolutions.* 2d ed. Chicago: University of Chicago Press.

Kumar, Krishan. 1976. "Industrialism and Post-Industrialism: Reflections on a Putative Transition." *Sociological Review* 24 (August): 439-78.

———. 1978. *Prophecy and Progress.* London: Penguin Books.

Kvavik, Robert B. 1976. *Interest Groups in Norwegian Politics.* Oslo: Universitets Førlaget.

Lakatos, Imre. 1970. "Falsification and the Methodology of Scientific Research Programmes." Pp. 91-196 in *Criticism and the Growth of Knowledge,* ed. Imre Lakatos and Alan Musgrave. Cambridge: Cambridge University Press.

Lane, Robert E. 1970. *Political Thinking and Consciousness.* Chicago: Markham.

LaPorte, Todd, ed. 1975. *Organized Social Complexity: Challenge to Politics and Policy.* Princeton: Princeton University Press.

Lapping, Brian. 1970. "Which Social Services Can We Save?" Pp. 180-93 in *The Future of the Social Services,* ed. William A. Robson and Bernard Crick. London: Penguin Books.

Lasch, Christopher. 1972. "Toward a Theory of Post-industrial Society." Pp. 36-50 in *Politics in the Post-Welfare State,* ed. Donald Hancock and Gordon Sjoberg. New York: Columbia University Press.

Latham, Earl. 1952. *The Group Basis of Politics.* Ithaca, N.Y.: Cornell University Press.

Levy, Marian J. 1966. *Modernization and the Structure of Societies.* Princeton: Princeton University Press.

Lewis, Oscar. 1970. *La Vida.* New York: Random House.

Lijphart, Arend. 1969. *The Politics of Accommodation.* Berkeley: University of California Press.

———. 1971. "Comparative Politics and the Comparative Method." *American Political Science Review* 65 (September): 682–93.

———. 1975. "The Comparable-Cases Strategy in Comparative Research." *Comparative Political Studies* 8 (July): 158–77.

Lindblom, Charles E. 1977. *Politics and Markets.* New York: Basic Books.

Local Government Act, 1972. 1972. London: Her Majesty's Stationery Office.

Local Government in England. 1972. London: Her Majesty's Stationery Office.

Local Government Operational Research Unit. 1968. *Performance and Size of Local Education Authorities.* Research Study 5. London: Her Majesty's Stationery Office.

Loveman, Brian. 1976. *Struggle in the Countryside, Politics and Rural Labor in Chile, 1919–1973.* Bloomington: Indiana University Press.

Lowi, Theodore J. 1969. *The End of Liberalism.* New York: W. W. Norton & Co.

McCaughrin, Craig. 1976. "An Ahistoric View of Revolution." *American Journal of Political Science* 20 (November): 637–52.

McConnell, Grant. 1966. *Private Power and American Democracy.* New York: Alfred A. Knopf.

Maisel, Richard. 1973. "The Decline of Mass Media." *Public Opinion Quarterly* 37 (Summer): 159–70.

Mallaby Committee. 1967. *The Staffing of Local Government.* London: Her Majesty's Stationery Office.

Marsh, Alan. 1975. "The 'Silent Revolution,' Value Priorities, and the Quality of Life in Britain." *American Political Science Review* 69 (March): 21–30.

Maslow, Abraham H. 1954. *Motivation and Personality.* New York: Harper & Row.

Maud Committee. 1967. *The Management of Local Government.* London: Her Majesty's Stationery Office.

Maxwell, Nicholas. 1974. "The Rationality of Scientific Discovery. II. An Aim Oriental Theory of Scientific Discovery." *Philosophy of Science* 4 (September): 227–47.

Meckstroth, Theodore W. 1974. "Some Problems in Cross-Level Inference." *American Journal of Political Science* 18 (February):

45-66.

———. 1975. "Most Different Systems and Most Similar Systems: A Study in the Logic of Comparative Inquiry." *Comparative Political Studies* 8 (July): 132-57.

Milbrath, Lester. 1965. *Political Participation.* Chicago: Rand McNally.

Miller, George. 1956. "The Magic Number Seven, Plus or Minus Two." *Psychological Review* 63 (January): 81-97.

Miller, Sidal M.; Riessman, Frank; and Seagull, Arthur A. 1965. "Poverty and Self-Indulgence: A Critique of the Non-deferred Gratification Pattern." Pp. 285-302 in *Poverty in America,* ed. Louis A. Ferman, Joyce L. Kornbluh, and Alan Haber. Ann Arbor: University of Michigan Press.

Mischel, T. 1966. "Pragmatic Aspects of Explanation." *Philosophy of Science* 33:41-59.

Mishan, E. J. 1972. *Elements of Cost-Benefit Analysis.* London: George Allen & Unwin.

Mitchell, B. R. 1975. *European Historical Statistics.* New York: Columbia University Press.

Moon, J. Donald. 1975. "The Logic of Political Inquiry: A Synthesis of Opposed Perspectives." Pp. 131-228 in *Handbook of Political Science,* vol. 1, ed. Fred I. Greenstein and Nelson W. Polsby. Reading, Mass.: Addison-Wesley.

Moore, Barrington, Jr. 1965. *Political Power and Social Theory.* New York: Harper & Row.

Moore, Wilbert E. 1963. "The Strategy of Fostering Performance and Responsibility." Pp. 231-42 in *Social Aspects of Economic Development in Latin America,* ed. Egbert de Vries and J. M. Echavarría. vol. 1. Paris: UNESCO.

Nakane, Chie. 1971. *Japanese Society.* Berkeley: University of California Press.

Nie, Norman H.; Powell, G. Bingham, Jr.; and Prewitt, Kenneth. 1969. "Social Structure and Political Participation: Developmental Relationships." *American Political Science Review* 60 (June): 361-78, (September): 808-32.

Nozick, Robert. 1974. *Anarchy, State and Utopia.* New York: Basic Books.

O'Connor, James. 1973. *The Fiscal Crisis of the State.* New York: St. Martin's Press.

Ollman, Bert. 1976. *Alienation.* London: Oxford University Press.

Olson, Mancur. 1965. *The Logic of Collective Action.* Cambridge, Mass.: Harvard University Press.

———. 1969. "The Principle of 'Fiscal Equivalence': The Division of Responsibilities among Different Levels of Government." *American Economic Review: Papers and Proceedings* 59 (May): 479-87.

Orbell, John, and Uno, Toro. 1972. "A Theory of Neighborhood Problem Solving: Political Action vs. Residential Mobility." *American Political Science Review* 66 (June): 471-89.

Ostrom, Elinor; Parks, Robert B.; and Whitaker, Gordon P. 1973. "Do We Really Want to Consolidate Urban Police Forces? A Reappraisal of Some Old Assertions." *Public Administration Review* 33 (September-October): 423-33.

Ostrom, Vincent. 1972. "Polycentricity." Paper delivered at the annual meeting of the American Political Science Association, Washington, D.C., September.

———, ed. 1974. "The Study of Federalism at Work." *Publius* 4 (Fall): 1-138.

Ostrom, Vincent, and Ostrom, Elinor. 1971. "Public Choice: A Different Approach to the Study of Public Administration." *Public Administration Review* 31 (March-April): 203-16.

Ostrom, Vincent; Tiebout, C. M.; and Warren, R. 1961. "The Organization of Government in Metropolitan Areas: A Theoretical Inquiry." *American Political Science Review* 60 (December): 831-42.

O'Toole, James. 1974. *Work and the Quality of Life: Resource Papers for Work in America.* Cambridge, Mass.: M.I.T. Press.

Panitch, Leo. 1977. "The Development of Corporatism in Liberal Democracies." *Comparative Political Studies* 10 (April): 61-90.

Partch, Richard D. 1976. "Toward a Spatial Theory of Intra-Nation Modernization in Advanced Societies: The West German Case, 1965-1969." *Zeitschrift für Soziologie* 5 (January): 52-69.

Pechman, Joseph A. 1975. "Making Economic Policy: The Role of the Economist." Pp. 23-78 in *Policies and Policy Making,* ed. Fred I. Greenstein and Nelson W. Polsby. Vol. 6 of *Handbook of Political Science.* Reading, Mass.: Addison-Wesley.

Polsby, Nelson W. 1963. *Community Power and Political Theory.* New Haven: Yale University Press.

Popper, Karl. 1970. "Normal Science and Its Dangers." Pp. 51-58 in *Criticism and the Growth of Knowledge,* ed. Imre Lakatos and Alan Musgrave. Cambridge: Cambridge University Press.

Przeworski, Adam. 1975. "Institutionalization of Voting Patterns, or Is Mobilization the Source of Decay?" *American Political Science Review* 69 (March): 49-67.

Przeworski, Adam, and Sprague, John. 1971. "Concepts in Search of Explicit Formulation: A Study in Measurement." *Midwest*

Journal of Political Science 15 (May): 183–218.

Przeworski, Adam, and Teune, Henry. 1970. *The Logic of Comparative Social Inquiry*. New York: John Wiley & Sons.

Putnam, Robert D. 1973. *The Beliefs of Politicians: Ideology, Conflict and Democracy in Britain and Italy.* New Haven: Yale University Press.

Rawls, John. 1971. *A Theory of Justice.* Cambridge, Mass.: Belkap Press of Harvard University Press.

Reform of Local Government in England. 1970. London: Her Majesty's Stationery Office.

Research Services, Ltd. 1969. *Community Attitudes Survey: England.* Research Study 9. London: Her Majesty's Stationery Office.

Richards, Peter C. 1973. *The Reformed Local Government System* London: George Allen & Unwin.

Riker, William, and Ordeshook, Peter. 1972. *Introduction to Positive Political Theory.* Englewood Cliffs, N.J.: Prentice-Hall, Inc.

Robbins, Lionel. [1932] 1973. *An Essay on the Nature and Significance of Economic Science.* London: Macmillan Co.

Rose, Richard, and Peter, B. Guy. "The Growth of Government and Political Bankruptcy: The Political Consequences of Economic Overload." Paper presented at the Midwest Political Science Meetings, Chicago, April.

Royal Commission on the Distribution of Income and Wealth. 1975. London: Her Majesty's Stationery Office.

Royal Commission on Local Government in England. 1969. 3 vols. Report of the Redcliffe-Maud Committee. London: Her Majesty's Stationery Office.

Ruggie, John C. 1972. "Collective Goods and Future International Collaboration." *American Political Science Review* 66 (September): 874–93.

Rummel, Rudolf. 1970. *Applied Factor Analysis.* Evanston, Ill.: Northwestern University Press.

Samuelson, Paul A. 1967. "Indeterminacy of Governmental Role in Public-Good Theory." *Papers in Non-Market Decision Making* 3 (Fall): 47.

Schmitter, Philippe C. 1971. *Interest Conflict and Political Change in Brazil.* Stanford, Calif.: Stanford University Press.

———. 1974. "Still the Century of Corporatism?" Pp. 85–131 in *The New Corporatism,* ed. Frederick B. Pike and Thomas Stritch. Notre Dame, Ind.: University of Notre Dame Press.

———. 1977. "Modes of Interest Intermediation and Models of Societal Change in Western Europe." *Comparative Political*

Studies 10 (April): 7–38.

Schwartz, Bernard, and Wade, H. W. R. 1972. *Legal Control of Government: Administrative Law in Britain and the United States.* Oxford: Clarendon Press.

Scitovsky, Tibor. 1976. *The Joyless Economy.* New York: Oxford University Press.

Self, Peter. 1975. "Economic Ideas and Government Operations." *Political Studies* 23 (June–September): 381–89.

Sen, A. K. 1966. "Peasants and Dualism with or without Surplus Labor." *Journal of Political Economy* 74 (October): 425–50.

Senior, Derek. 1969. *Memorandum of Dissent.* Report of the Royal Commission on Local Government, vol. 2. London: Her Majesty's Stationery Office.

Shively, W. Phillips. 1972. "Voting Stability and the Nature of Party Attachments in the Weimar Republic." *American Political Science Review* 66 (December): 1203–25.

Shonfield, Andrew. 1965. *Modern Capitalism.* London: Oxford University Press.

Silverman, S. F. 1968. "Agricultural Organization, Social Structure and Values in Italy: Amoral Familism Reconsidered." *American Anthropologist* 70 (February): 1-21.

Simon, Herbert. 1969. *The Sciences of the Artificial.* Cambridge, Mass.: M.I.T. Press.

Skeffington, Arthur. 1969. *People and Planning.* London: Her Majesty's Stationery Office.

Sproule-Jones, Mark. 1972. "Strategic Tensions in the Scale of Political Analysis." *British Journal of Political Science* 2, pt. 2 (April): 172–91.

Storer, Norman W. 1966. *The Social System of Science.* New York: Holt, Rinehart & Winston.

Taylor, Charles L., and Hudson, Michael C. 1972. *World Handbook of Social and Political Indicators. II.* New Haven: Yale University Press.

Taylor, Ian R., and Taylor, Laurie, eds. 1973. *Politics and Deviance.* Harmondsworth, Middx.: Penguin Books.

Taylor, Michael. 1976. *Anarchy and Cooperation.* New York: John Wiley & Sons.

Teune, Henry. 1975. "Comparative Research, Experimental Design, and the Comparative Method." *Comparative Political Studies* 8 (July): 195–99.

Tipps, Dean C. 1973. "Modernization Theory and the Comparative Study of Societies: A Critical Perspective." *Comparative Studies in Society and History* 15 (March): 199–226.

Tisdale, Clem A. 1975. "Concepts of Rationality in Economics." *Philosophy of the Social Sciences* 5 (September): 259–72.

Touraine, Alain. 1974. *The Post-industrial Society.* London: Wildwood House.

Tullock, Gordon. 1965. *The Politics of Bureaucracy.* Washington, D.C.: Public Affairs Press.

Truman, David B. 1951. *The Governmental Process.* New York: Alfred A. Knopf.

Tufte, Edward R. 1978. *Political Control of the Economy.* Princeton: Princeton University Press.

United Nations Statistical Yearbook. 1974. New York: U.N. Department of Economic and Social Affairs Statistical Office.

United States Bureau of the Census. 1970. *Historical Statistics.* Washington, D.C.: Government Printing Office.

Valentine, Charles A. 1968. *Culture and Poverty: Critique and Counter-Proposals.* Chicago: University of Chicago Press.

Watanuki, Joji. 1973. "Japanese Politics: Changes, Continuities, and Unknowns." Institute of International Relations Research Paper, Series A-16. Tokyo: Sophia University.

Waterbury, Robert. 1975. "Non-revolutionary Peasants: Oaxaca Compared to Morelos in the Mexican Revolution." *Comparative Studies in Society and History* 17 (October): 410–42.

Wheatley Commission. 1969. *The Reform of Local Government in Scotland.* London: Her Majesty's Stationery Office.

Whyte, William. 1957. *The Organization Man.* Garden City, N.Y.: Doubleday Anchor Books.

Williams, Emil. 1970. "Peasantry and City: Cultural Resistance and Change in Historical Perspective—a European Case." *American Anthropologist* 72 (June): 528–44.

Williams, Oliver P. 1971. *Metropolitan Political Analysis: A Social Access Approach.* New York: Free Press.

———. 1976. "Toward a Theory of Comparative Urban Politics." Paper prepared for the International Workshop, Comparative Ecological Analysis of Social Change, University of Ljubljiana, August 1–12.

Wilson, James Q., and Banfield, Edward C. 1964. "Public-Regardingness as a Value Premise in Voting Behavior." *American Political Science Review* 58 (December): 886.

Winkler, J. T. 1977. "The Coming Corporation." Pp. 78–87 in *The End of the Keynesian Era,* ed. Robert Skidelsky. London: Macmillan Co.

Wise, John, and Yotopoulos, Pan A. 1969. "The Empirical Content of Economic Rationality: A Test for a Less Developed Economy."

Journal of Political Economy 77 (November-December): 976-1004.

Woolf, M. 1968. *Local Authority Services and the Characteristics of Administrative Areas.* Research Study 5. London: Her Majesty's Stationery Office.

Wright, Erik Olin. 1978. *Class, Crisis and State.* London: NLB.

Yamane, Taro. 1973. *Statistics: An Introductory Analysis.* New York: Harper & Row.

Young, Forrest W. 1963. *Cojoint Scaling.* Chapel Hill: University of North Carolina L. L. Thurstone Psychometric Laboratory.

Index